STUDIO 44
ARCHITECTS

INTRODUCTION BY
AARON BETSKY

TEXTS BY
HANS IBELINGS

EDITED BY
GEORGI STANISHEV

STUDIO 44
ARCHITECTS

CONCEPTS • STRATEGIES • WORKS

**NEW FORMS FOR RUSSIA'S
CONTEMPORARY CITIES**

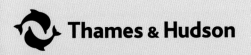

First published in the United Kingdom in 2017 by Thames & Hudson Ltd,
181A High Holborn, London WC1V 7QX

Studio 44 Architects: Buildings and Projects © 2017 Thames & Hudson Ltd, London

Texts © 2017 their respective authors
Photographs © 2017 Studio 44 Architects unless otherwise stated
Illustrations © 2017 Studio 44 Architects unless otherwise stated

Text editor: Lyudmila Likhacheva
Picture editor: Margarita Yawein
Translator: Olga Glotova
Coordinator: Daria Nikiforova

Jacket and book design: Peter Dawson, Namkwan Cho, www.gradedesign.com

British Library Cataloguing-in-Publication Data
A catalogue record for this book is available from the British Library

ISBN 978-0-500-34309-8

Printed and bound in Slovenia by DZS-Grafik d.o.o.

To find out about all our publications, please visit **www.thamesandhudson.com**.
There you can subscribe to our e-newsletter, browse or download our current
catalogue, and buy any titles that are in print.

CONTENTS

INTRODUCTION

Studio 44: Monument Makers

Aaron Betsky   7

ANALYSIS

An Abundance of Architecture

Hans Ibelings   9

INTERVIEW

Introduction: Dialogue as a Form of Thought

Georgi Stanishev   19

Nikita Yawein Interviewed by Oleg Yawein   20

WORKS   34

EARLY WORKS   36

The Cube Residential Estate   39

A Home for Three Generations of One Family   43

Signal Children's Pioneer Camp   47

Amphitheatre of Boxes   51

EXPLORATION OF THE RUSSIAN NORTH   56

Kremlin Housing Community   59

Nursery School Building, Kremlin Housing Community   65

Solovki Airport Hotel   69

Yaweins' Country House   75

ST PETERSBURG AT THE
TURN OF THE 21ST CENTURY   80

Central Branch of Sberbank of Russia, St Petersburg   83

Ladozhsky Railway Station   93

Residential Building, Krestyansky Lane   105

Nevsky 38 Business Centre   109

Residential Building, 10th Sovietskaya Street   121

Studio 44 Offices   127

Linkor Business Centre   133

New Peterhof Hotel   141

21ST-CENTURY PROJECTS AND BUILDINGS   146

The State Hermitage Museum in the East Wing
of the General Staff Building   149

Astana Railway Station   175

Palace of Schoolchildren   181

Zhastar Youth Palace   193

Football Stadium for 2018 Fifa World Cup   201

Olympic Park Railway Station   207

Tsar's Garden Hotel Complex   219

Science and Technology Museum   227

Campus of Graduate School of Management,
St Petersburg University   239

Boris Eifman Dance Academy   251

CITY CENTRES   262

High-Rise Buildings near Ladozhsky Railway Station   265

City on the Water: Residential District in Coastal Area   273

Residential Quarter on Oktyabrskaya Embankment   277

Centre of Modern Culture at New Holland   283

Development Concept for Konyushennaya and North Kolomna
Neighbourhoods in Historical Centre of St Petersburg   295

Concept for the Development of the Historical   301
Centre of Kaliningrad

About Studio 44   313

List of Completed Projects   315

Project Credits   316

Picture Credits   319

INTRODUCTION

STUDIO 44: MONUMENT MAKERS

Aaron Betsky

It is difficult to make monumental architecture these days. If the designing of grand structures for the state, or for those who could afford the means to create imposing forms, was once at the core of the discipline, today we want our buildings to be friendly, open and flexible. At the same time, few entities or individuals have the ability to pay for anything but the minimum investment in a building, and thus anything big and expressive is seen as wasteful. On a more theoretical level, the notion that we should build for the ages is difficult to support in an era in which the use of natural resources should be kept to a minimum, and where participation in our institutions, companies and other structures is to be welcomed.

One of the few firms that is still creating monumental architecture is St Petersburg's Studio 44. Over the last few decades, it has built up a practice that is founded in monuments and monumentality. Using an eclectic set of approaches and styles, it has sought to find ways to re-imbue the institutions and even structures of everyday life with a sense of import and meaning. Abstracting the classic techniques of monument making, which sought to impress us with scale, materials, rhythmic sequences of spaces, sculptural presence and historic references, the firm designs buildings that, at their best, are able to awe.

Partially, Studio 44 is able to do so because of where it works, since Russia is one of the few countries that is still seeking to secure state power in buildings. Partially, it is successful in its approach because of its commissions, which include the renovation of already monumental buildings for uses that tap into such grand traditions, as well as large railway stations and commercial structures. But, in addressing these tasks, it has figured out how to combine modernist and classicizing tendencies to create an approach that makes the most out of its situation.

That Studio 44 has its roots in the design of large housing projects and infrastructure, something that dates in part back to the practice of the founding partners' father, means that it is well schooled in handling a mass of people with large yet efficient structures, as well as with spaces that can accommodate them, but which can also help them understand where they are and where they are going. The aesthetic developed by the firm – industrial elements cleaned up and abstracted, rooted in masonry forms and organized using modern flow diagrams – recalls the grandeur of such points of arrival and departure while working in the manner required by such places today. It is at the heart of its best architecture for other programmes.

Studio 44's training in the Soviet and post-Soviet (postmodern) era also gives it a predilection towards solid forms, superstructures and monuments that are larger than life and intended to be imposing. In its best work, however, it is able to temper and moderate these structures into something lighter, not only in terms of mass but also in terms of how it brings daylight into the structures. The designers at Studio 44 are not nostalgic, but seek to give the complex and more ephemeral projects with which they are confronted, from schools to hotels, a more complete and solid realization.

Studio 44 is able to preserve the past – both literally, when it works on restorations and renovations, and in its designs. It is also able to open up structures to current needs while adding architecture that is wholly its own. Its designs use geometry, axial and symmetrical alignments (although sometimes broken or modified), and materials that invite touch while appearing solid, as well as compositions that articulate different programme elements in balance with one another, to achieve a sense of clarity, beauty and a modern monumentality.

ANALYSIS

AN ABUNDANCE OF ARCHITECTURE

Hans Ibelings

'No artist will better compress speech to conciseness than he who has skill to enrich the same with as varied an ornamentation as possible.' Desiderius Erasmus, *Copia* (1512).

There is no typical Studio 44 architecture. Or at least not if the notion of the typical is based on its visual appearance. While the work of many architects and architectural offices is recognizable because of their consistent idioms, recurrent motifs and stable preferences for certain forms and materials, the idiosyncrasy of the work of Studio 44 resides in an intriguing absence of such a recognizability. It is not easy to discern immediately, for instance, that the Kremlin housing on the Solovetsky Islands (1) is designed by the same office that conceived the Palace of Schoolchildren in Astana (2), even if the time that passed between the first and the second project is taken into account. The same is true for more recent works as well, such as the Boris Eifman Dance Academy in St Petersburg (3) and the Sochi railway station (4). The same applies to the office's urban-planning projects, which use very different design approaches, sometimes adhering to strict grid systems of perimeter blocks (5), particularly where urbanity is created ex novo, and sometimes sensitively and partially invisibly intervening in the existing urban fabric, such as in the development concept for St Petersburg's Konyushennaya and North Kolomna neighbourhoods (6).

The rich diversity of Studio 44's architecture and urbanism should not be mistaken for inconsistency or lack of rigour. Rather, it reflects a method of design that distinguishes the conceptual point of departure from its outward appearance. This is comparable with the idea of linguist Noam Chomsky

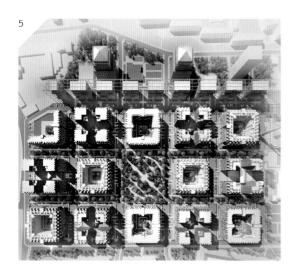

that there is a distinction in languages between deep and surface structures. The surface structure of Studio 44's architecture has many and diverse manifestations, but underneath this diversity is a solidly consistent deep structure. To put it differently, one could say that Studio 44 founder Nikita Yawein and his brother Oleg combine strong intellectual backbones with remarkably mercurial mindsets, leading to an ongoing exploration of new and untried architectural expressions, without deserting the core principles behind the work.

Clearly, Studio 44 is able to master multiple architectural vocabularies. Some of the work takes its cues from advanced technologies, while others explore traditional crafts of folklore and vernacular; some works are loaded with easily accessible symbolic references, while others refrain from this and display a restraint abstractness. This architectural eloquence reminds one of what Dutch philosopher Desiderius Erasmus of Rotterdam recommended in his treatise *De Utraque Verborum ac Rerum Copia*, first published in 1512. This treatise offers a method for appropriate and entertaining speech and writing. Erasmus's text has more than one English translation, and is published under different titles, one being *Copia of Words and Ideas*, and another *Copia: Foundations of the Abundant Style*. That there is more than one title for the translation of Erasmus's treatise underscores what the author claims; namely, that a speaker of merit can say everything in more than one way, in a multitude of different ways. According to Erasmus, this talent should be honed by practising abundance, which he elucidated by showing how many variations there are for such a simple sentence as 'Your letter has delighted me very much', from a scant 'Not unpleasing to me was your letter', to a very generous 'You would scarcely believe what a multitude of joys your letter brought to my spirit.'

The simultaneously humorous and serious text of Erasmus (allegedly the inspiration for Raymond Queneau's *Exercises in Style*) should be interpreted not as an encouragement to say the same over and over again in slightly different ways, as Erasmus did with his single sentence, but as an argument for appropriate variation, which may be mastered only by those who can say both a lot and almost nothing: 'For as far as conciseness of speech is concerned, who could speak more tersely than he who has ready at hand an extensive array of words and figures for conciseness?' To this Erasmus added: 'No one certainly will see more quickly and more surely what can be suitably omitted than he who has seen what can be added and in what ways' (which is a variation of the epigraph at the beginning of this piece).

The work of Studio 44 displays a comparable capacity to add and to omit, and to produce architecture that is either evocatively ornate or suggestively abstract. In this respect, Studio 44 differs from the many architectural offices that offer only one vocabulary. A majority of architects is in this sense like Giorgio Morandi, a great artist who time and time again meticulously studied the magnificent play of the same few volumes, brought together in light: a couple of bottles, a pitcher, a box and a bowl. At the other end of the spectrum is a much smaller group of architects, including the Yaweins, who are more comparable to Francis Picabia, who relentlessly explored different subjects, themes, media and styles in his artistic work.

In its mastery of multiple rhetorical figures of design, Studio 44's position could be characterized as post-postmodern, overcoming the alleged opposition between modernism and postmodernism, which has become perhaps the most ossified cliché of recent architectural history and criticism. Seen through the lenses of modernism and postmodernism, some of the works of Studio 44 are apparently directly related to the modernist ideals of innovation in form, materials and building technology, while others can be seen as postmodern, harking back to premodern or vernacular traditions, underlining the narrative, communicative aspects of buildings. Some, however, do both at the same time, such as the Linkor Business Centre (7), which contains several naval metaphors, from the hull shape of the building to the seagull-like elements hanging in the main lobby, but which simultaneously expresses a supermodern sophistication in materials and technology. The same is true for the Tsar's Garden Hotel (8), which references both contemporary and historical sources.

If in the world of art and architecture the certainties of modernism were replaced by postmodernism's equally

7

8

9

10

assured anti-modern relativism, the now prevailing post-postmodernist state is closer to an almost indifferent impartiality. Evidently, this comes closer to 'anything goes' than anything that was conceived during the period of postmodernism, which gave the motto currency.

It might be too far-fetched to relate this post-postmodernism in the work of Studio 44 to a larger scheme of things, but there is at least a parallel between this stance and the Russian society in which the studio emerged, which had seen the rather abrupt demise of one the strongest ideologies of the twentieth century. In a short period, Russia morphed from post-socialist to a complicated ex-socialist condition, which could equally be called post-post-socialist. In many ways, the Russian context in which Studio 44 worked and works is a place where indeed anything – or sometimes nothing – goes, a very complex and contradictory place, ruthlessly capitalist, but not without nostalgia for the most ruthless of Soviet leaders; patriotic at a time when Russia is much more globalized than it ever was during the Soviet times of international socialism. These contradictions illustrate an aspect of a post-ideological world, in which opposites have lost much of their antithetical character, because everything is accepted and assessed in its own terms.

This applies to the work of Studio 44 as well. In the office's architecture, the way a building looks can be disconnected from both its context and its programme. This can be illustrated by comparing Ladozhsky railway station (9) in St Petersburg with the towers (10) designed a few years later for the same area, and with two other stations of Studio 44.

Ladozhsky station has obviously taken its cues from the railway palaces of the nineteenth century, which were themselves often steel-and-glass versions of Caracalla's baths in Rome. In this respect, it reminds one of Aldo Rossi's notion of autonomy, of architectural types that are able to accommodate different programmes without changing their form, withstanding functional determinism. More than anything else, Ladozhsky station is conceived as a building with its own logic, apparently not dictated by the pragmatism of its programmatic and infrastructural requirements. In other words, it is a building with a deliberately static form, which resists the pressures exercised on every station, including this one, as a nexus of flows of people and modes of transportation. Just like New York's Grand Central Terminal, Ladozhsky station is first and foremost a place and a space, one that does not emphasize that the complex is an infrastructural hub for different forms of public and private transportation.

The comparison with Rossi's idea of typology is not accidental here; in plan, there is a striking parallel between the station and some of Rossi's projects, including his famous San Cataldo Cemetery in Modena. While Rossi imposed his rationalist order on such relatively simple and malleable programmes as a graveyard, Studio 44 has managed to put a comparable approach into practice in a far more complex situation of a train and bus station on a small site.

Right next to the station, Studio 44 has proposed a completely different project: a high-rise ensemble comprising five soaring, crystal-like objects. This project is not only unlike anything else in the neighbourhood, but also unlike any other design of Studio 44. While the station manages to induce a shock of recognition, the towers offer a 'shock of the new'. Even though they are directly next to each another in the very same St Petersburg setting, the architecture of these two projects is completely different – even, at first sight, irreconcilably so. Yet on closer inspection they appear to be determined by a comparable confidence in the structuring logic of geometry. The station is based on an axial symmetry, which is palpable everywhere in and around the building. The five towers suggest that their shapes and position are random; in plan, however, they seem to be forming a near-symmetrical order.

Aside from Ladozhsky station, Studio 44 has designed two other railway stations: one in Astana, and one in Sochi, the latter having been built on the occasion of the 2014 Winter Olympics. Each station is completely different. The St Petersburg station is playing on conventional railway-station typologies; the Astana station (11) is dominated by a monumental, transparent hyperbolic paraboloid roof, which seems to build on the engineering traditions of (late) modernism; and the Olympic Park station in Sochi is a dynamic reflection of traffic movements, capable of being read as an architectural flow diagram.

This double comparison, of Ladozhsky station with a high-rise project for the same area, and with two other programmatically related projects elsewhere, offers at least two insights. The first is that contextualism, even if it is seriously taken into account, is not the main driver behind the architecture of Studio 44; the second is that there is no functionalist idea of 'form follows function', as shown by the stations, which are three completely different buildings for essentially very similar programmes. Each individual work of Studio 44 follows its own internal logic, and has a unique architectural expression and spatial articulation. However, underneath every work is a coherent design approach. No matter how complex the eventual building, the essence is always a rigorous, systematic concept. This logic can be an elementary geometry inscribed in the plan or section; a structure of repetitive geometric forms of different scales; or a clear contour that determines the perimeter of the intervention. So this, perhaps, is what characterizes the work of Studio 44 and sets it apart from other architectural offices: that it is diverse on the surface, but unified by a strong logic under its skin.

In many of the earliest works there is a clear emphasis on structure not dissimilar to the repetitive patterns of Western European structuralism, championed by the likes of Herman Hertzberger, or metabolism, professed by such Japanese architects as Kiyonori Kikutake and Kisho Kurokawa. Yet, as demonstrated particularly by the projects that predate the establishment of Studio 44, this interest in structure is driven less by the wish to create buildings that in theory could be extended in every direction, and more by a desire to establish a definite, and definitive, form. Projects like the Cube, A Home for Three Generations of One Family, the Signal Children's Pioneer Camp (12) and the Amphitheatre of Boxes (13) are exemplary illustrations of how patterns, and repetitive forms, can actually structure architecture on different scales. These early Studio 44 works offer clues for reading the later projects as well, which in essence are almost always using, and sticking to, a geometrical starting point, albeit less often based on repetitive forms.

The strategy of basing a design on a geometrical point of departure is most convincing when Studio 44 is working within the existing context of urban fabrics, buildings and rooms, elevating incoherent or inconclusive settings to well-structured environments. This, for example, is visible in the renovations, conversions and extensions of existing buildings and neighbourhoods, such as the St Petersburg projects of the central branch of Sberbank (15), the Nevsky 38 Business Centre (14), the offices of Studio 44 itself, and the transformation of the East Wing of the General Staff Building (16) for the Hermitage Museum. In each case the interventions are structured by classical means of geometry to create a new spatial logic within the existing spaces or urban tissue – made-to-measure solutions for the specific requirements of each and every assignment.

Part of the specificity of every project resides in its siting. Even when Studio 44's contextualist attitude is never simply a matter of 'doing as the locals do', rarely does any work deliberately rupture the surroundings, or neglect the history of the site. Many projects are preceded and accompanied by meditations on the site's history and historical architecture. Cases in point are the projects made for the Solovetsky Islands: the housing project mentioned earlier, a nursery school and an airport hotel (19), all of which use the materials, forms and typologies of the islands' traditional architecture, blended with the geometrical order that characterizes so many of the office's projects. The same combination of vernacular elements and configurative repetition returns in the country house the Yawein brothers have designed for their family (17), and shows up in different guises in the New Peterhof Hotel (18) just outside St Petersburg, which found its place between the church and the residential architecture, and the Science and Technology Museum in Tomsk (20), which relates to Russian traditions of wood construction.

One possible explanation for the absence of attempts to subserviently blend the new with the old is that for Studio 44, there seems to be no categorical difference between them. This could also explain the seamless and frictionless alternation within the oeuvre, and often even within single projects, of modern, postmodern and vernacular elements.

This eclectic inclusiveness can be seen as postmodern, or even post-postmodern, but it can also be lifted out of an exclusive and rarefied cultural world and situated in a

Russian context, where the significance of architecture is not simply determined by the question of whether it looks contemporary or not. This is important to underline, because architectural criticism, and architectural history, often use the developments in Western (European) architecture as their main points of reference, tending to see architecture outside the West through a Western lens. The hometown of the Yaweins, St Petersburg, is on the cusp of different territories, being rather European and Western from a Russian perspective, but not completely Western and European in the eyes of Westerners and Europeans. For many Western Europeans, including many intellectuals, Russia, and its predecessor the Soviet Union, are deeply foreign places. This has a long history. As Larry Wolff has carefully analysed in *Inventing Eastern Europe: The Map of Civilization on the Mind of the Enlightenment*, published in 1994, an opposition between East and West succeeded the much older division of Europe between a cultivated South (that is, everything from the Roman Empire until the Italian city states of the Renaissance) and a barbarian North. With the shift of the continent's economic and cultural centre of gravity to the north-west, this division flipped to an opposition between a cultured West and a barbarian East. A good example of the Western vision of the East can be found in Marquis de Custine's dispatches from Russia – and from St Petersburg in particular – bundled in his 1842 publication *La Russie en 1839*. In this book, Custine came to the dismissive, and questionable, conclusion that Russia's culture was nothing more than a European veneer on top of what was, according to him, Asian. Even if Custine's conclusion exemplifies an incapacity to understand Russia, it underscores the idea that Russia was foreign. This idea continued to exist throughout the twentieth century, when Russia became the leading socialist republic within the USSR, and even today there is still this implication that, no matter what, Russia is a different place. Yet at the same time, from a Russian perspective, St Petersburg is in many ways much more European than any Russian city, and not only because it is geographically closer to Tallinn and Helsinki than to Moscow.

Being more-European-than-Russian, and more-Russian-than-European, has always given St Petersburg a very particular position, including in the history of architecture, and this might serve as a caveat that what looks the same from a Western perspective is not always the same in Russian eyes. So, even if some of the works of Studio 44 may look postmodern to Westerners, that does not mean that they are directly derived from the same sources as Western postmodernism, or completely understandable in postmodern terms. Likewise, Russian constructivism at the beginning of the twentieth century may have had similarities with the modern architecture that emerged simultaneously elsewhere in Europe, but it was definitely not the same. All this is to say that even if it is evident that the appearance of architecture is never accidental for Studio 44, it is neither a prescriptive, ideological matter. For Studio 44, architecture concerns the transmission of deeper principles of form and organization, which transcend ideology and style. It may be true that it is the tone that makes the music, but the work of Studio 44 reveals that the tone is not the music.

18

19
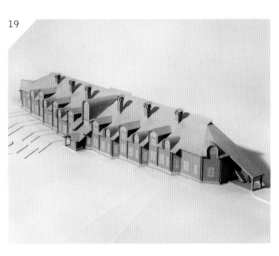

20

INTERVIEW

INTRODUCTION: DIALOGUE AS A FORM OF THOUGHT

Georgi Stanishev

Dialogue is one of the oldest ways of constructing concepts. In antiquity, dialogues were mastered to the point of becoming a literary genre that allowed philosophers to determine where they stood in their search for truth.

At the same time, dialogue works as a creative method, when discussion is aimed at finding a solution. Participants in such dialogues form dyads, well known in literature, science, politics, etc. It is known that they are effective when participants complement each other, like Holmes and Watson, like Deleuze and Guattari. It is especially apparent in architectural practice, where the compatibility of Sejima and Nishizawa or Herzog and de Meuron is grounded in the differences between styles of thought – given something of a common denominator, of course.

The collaboration between Nikita and Oleg Yawein is, undoubtedly, one of those dyads. However, it is based on their differences and unique characteristics that find room to coexist within the framework of a single cultural paradigm. This common platform, a common understanding of architectural motifs, goals and structure of architectural thought, has been developing within the Yawein family for a century. Here, we can truly talk about a professional dynasty, one that begins with Igor Yawein, the father of Nikita and Oleg, a most talented architect who, in the 1920s, shaped the unique nature of St Petersburg's constructivism. It is something of a genetic transmission of an architectural discourse between generations of one family, which results in a highly concentrated solution of architectural culture. It is curious that, despite inheriting the same profession, this genetic code drives the Yawein brothers to the far corners of the architectural field. Nikita is mainly a practitioner – driven, ambitious and business-like – who, at the same time, is very sensitive to the poetry in life and in architecture, and is ready to step up in defence of the fragile balance upholding the world. Probably, it was this sensitivity and the ability to balance various interests that helped Nikita Yawein in his work as Head of Committee for the Protection of Monuments, when, for many years, he was responsible for the strategy and tactics of preserving St Petersburg's unique architectural heritage. Oleg is an explorer of spatial logic and the limits of the world's architectural nature. Since the 1970s, he has been developing the potential of architectural theory by introducing a structural and semiotic view of the nature of artistic language.

Oleg and Nikita Yawein occupy opposite poles of the profession, and this creates the tension that makes dialogue meaningful, the impulses and currents that make any such dyad work. It is the basis of the family mythology, which assigns Nikita and Oleg different roles and even creates geographical distance between them. The brothers work independently and separately of each other: Nikita is in St Petersburg, where he runs Studio 44 Architects, one of Russia's largest and most influential architectural firms, while Oleg is in Moscow, where he is a professor of architecture, a theoretician and an architectural analyst. Despite all of this, the ongoing conversation witnessed by the reader in the interview below turns into an integral part of both architects' work, be it on purpose or by accident. Nikita's view of Oleg's theorizing often contains adjustments for practical issues; Oleg's view of Nikita's work discovers systemic approaches and ideological foundations that are often left subconscious.

The Hermitage XXI project (see page 149), in which the Yawein dyad tested their collaboration in real work, lies on the foundation of juxtaposition and synergy of two types of architectural consciousness. The project's space is so firmly introduced into the structure of the historic building exactly for this reason: it is grounded in the intense dialogue between the two opposites, between the pragmatic and the theoretical, the poetic and the conceptual.

The systemic approach in the work of Nikita and Studio 44 Architects, as Oleg sees it, is not just a grammar of form, but a system of constructing space aimed at achieving balance between the acting forces, directions of movement and functional goals. It is a projection of a world model grounded in the balance of chaos and order, regularity and spontaneity, necessity and freedom.

Oleg Yawein Recently, you and I have stopped talking about architecture. Of course, we talk about specific projects and what needs to be done there. You cannot really do without conversations like that. But talking about architecture just for the sake of talking about architecture, you know, with a glass of wine, but completely seriously, now seems like bad manners: words sound fake and ostentatious, and the conversation stumbles or veers off into another topic. But questions about the nature of your architecture do arise and grow in number – and I am not the only one asking them.

You build a lot, really a lot, and you work within the context of the time, place and people's preferences, but it is not popular architecture in any way. You seem to be in the crowd, but you are always on your own. There are plenty of concepts and architectural legends in the competition works of Studio 44, but I always thought that, for you, conceptuality is an architectural material, just like specifications of brick. You are not a conceptual architect and in no way are you a 'paper architect'. In my opinion, you are, actually, an 'anti-paper architect': even in drawings that are impossible to realize, even in the most abstract schemes, your design thought is quite the opposite to 'paper architecture'. It looks like you very purposefully distance yourself from what we call 'mainstream' and what many see as a guideline, as the height of civilization and its future. To me, it looks as if, for you, this height is more like a competing firm. You have a whole portfolio of work devoted to local architectural traditions. I took part in some of these projects and I am confident that they have never had anything to do with architectural regionalism. However, it is somehow very hard for me to explain. Could you? It is unclear to me to what genre or to what movement your architecture belongs. It is as if you followed too many architectural styles – or none at all. On the other hand, you definitely have a system of your own: everyone feels that it is there and it is often pointed out. However, nobody can say what the system is, and if they start talking about it, they end up saying platitudes or ridiculous intellectualisms. Can you try and explain? Just do not talk about function, form, environmental approach and the like. And try not to repeat any of the things you had said at urban development councils, in government

reports, interviews or at architectural events. Here and now, you don't have to persuade anybody; it is just a chance to think things over and, maybe, formulate the way your architecture is made.

Nikita Yawein You know, we were brought up in an environment seeped in constructivist ideas, with literature and masterpieces from those times. There were a lot of works on the history of architecture. In all the architectural material that surrounded us, I was not interested in some stylistic points – I did not even get their meaning, and I still do not get it. I was always interested in the construction of a building, not as a Lego toy, but as a complex mechanism based not on technical but on cultural origins.

When I was in my second year of studies, I was very much impressed by Le Corbusier's 'House of Villas', where a small house with a garden is accepted as a starter unit, and the architect stacks them and lines them up, and, as a result, puts together a house with gardens the way you would put together a shelving unit. Later, I became awfully interested in all those units where the floor levels in the living room, kitchen and bedroom were higher or lower than each other. Ginzburg has very compact and very complex units of this kind. As for Unité d'Habitation in Marseille, when I was a student, I found its starter unit too simple, uninteresting even, while more complex constructions based on semi-levels always seemed intriguing. If we continue this topic, Melnikov's club in Stromynka Street, where three halls face one hall – that's interesting. And it's even more interesting when five round halls in the Zuev Worker's Club project, also by Melnikov, can be unified into one. For me, all of those buildings are 'constructs', but they are all based on some scheme that is derivative from a person.

O.Y. It would be great if you described an early project of yours, preferably in simple and clear terms.

N.Y. The Cube, a competition design, which was one of my first experiments in spatial constructions based on starter units.[1] The basic spatial unit developed in this project consisted of three cubic modules ($3 \times 3 \times 3$ m), and one of them was

---

1 See page 39.
   ARCHITECT: Nikita Yawein

higher by half (4.5 m). The spatial design of the unit was merged with the structural one. The stairwell fit inside the same module comprised of two cubes (6 × 3 m). The combinations of modular units around nuclei containing daytime rooms of sesquialtera height produced a variety of apartment types: small, medium and large. Using those spatial models for apartments, I began putting together buildings in such a way that the sesquialtera-height nuclei also had upper side lighting. The 'Anthill' building was the result of assembling different apartments around a stairwell. A linear composition yielded buildings that came down the slope in picturesque steps. It is interesting that, with every initial type of apartment, there was only one reasonable way of assembly, which practically had no alternatives, although the result could appear to be a free composition or a picturesque mountain of building blocks. The outcome was a diverse and dense building fabric with small courtyards of variable section, pedestrian streets, and very compact layered structures.

O.Y. I always thought that your constructs had a characteristic feature: the spatial structure is a construction, a functional unit and a symbol. For this merger, I think the Signal Children's Pioneer Camp is the most illustrative, if not programmatic.[2] Here, the rational assembly of functional units in a ravine produces a spatial model for the structure of a pioneer camp. I remember very well how you cut the huge cardboard mock-up at night, after work, and I was scolded for supposedly encouraging you in your architectural maximalism and thus assisting in the ruin of your health. But to understand how function, structure and symbolism come together in this project, you have to at least know what a pioneer camp is.

N.Y. The functional typology of Young Pioneers' camps is hardly known in the West, I think; even here it is quite forgotten, though, in essence, the Young Pioneers' Organization was a Soviet version of the Boy Scout Movement. The initial functional unit in the camp was a pioneer detachment, that is, about thirty teenagers and a mentor. Each detachment lived its own, relatively separate life. At the same time, a Young Pioneers' camp was a single community. Togetherness was regulated and asserted through repeated rituals. All sorts of processes and events in a Young Pioneers' camp began and ended with a ceremonial line-up. Camps could have different layouts, but the line-up, where every detachment had its own place, was a kind of a canonical mini-model of the whole camp community. Another place that brought everyone together was the bonfire. Every morning began with a line-up, and in the evening everyone gathered around a bonfire and sang songs.

O.Y. But there were plenty of Young Pioneers' camps built during the Soviet times: detachment blocks, canteen block, club, line-up square and sports grounds, distribution schemes for the rest of the programme. What did you use and what did you change?

N.Y. At Signal Camp, the project is assembled from the elements of the functional programme and from structural parts intended to stabilize the ground.

The site for the camp on the Black Sea was on a rather steep slope, with a ravine and a stream running towards the sea. The ravine was a big problem: there was a danger of landslides, especially in the spring, when the stream overflowed. A high probability of earthquakes made the problem even graver. So, the ravine needed either strengthening or filling.

I decided that the camp itself would act as a means to strengthen the ravine. The initial structural unit for the strengthening purpose was a single-storey detachment residential block. I came up with a 'cogged' linear layout, where the rooms faced the sea and were placed at an angle to the ravine axis. In addition to room orientation, corner ventilation and open space zoning, this idea yielded a structure that functioned as a single unit – symmetrical, rigid and ideal to meet the seismic requirements. Single-storey detachment buildings form terraces on the ravine slope and fit into each other like cogs. In the event of an earthquake, they would oscillate independently of each other, but, together, they reinforce the slope.

This structure had its own assembly logic. This logic had a will of its own. You have to feel and follow it, experiment with

---

2   See page 47.
    ARCHITECT: Nikita Yawein
    STRUCTURAL ENGINEER: Leonid Kaplan

it, explore its possibilities and limits. Sometimes it seems that the architect here acts only as intermediary.

The geometry of cogged joints results in the whole composition expanding from down up. The wings of the terraces on the top formed an enormous landscape theatre preventing landslides. Each level has two wings – two detachments of children of the same age. The higher and wider, the older the children. Young children would live below, closer to the centre, to the entrance and to the sea. Along the central axis, a gap, which widened at the top, was left to show off the stream. The axis is oriented towards the sea. At the bottom of the central axis, near the pedestrian and traffic entrance to the camp, there is a space for the ceremonial line-up. We played down the military parade qualities, which are so inherent to this function, and emphasized the idea of a theatre, where actors are spectators and spectators are actors. The line-up square was interpreted as 'a theatre of theatres', or a theatre where the whole camp settlement came together. It is an embryo, a model for the whole camp – the beginning and the end. The camp becomes an amphitheatre that grows out of a living, functioning theatre.

O.Y. At the time, many people pointed out that Signal Camp reminded them of pueblos, Native American settlements that also often cling to mountain slopes, while their flat roofs serve as terraces for houses higher up. But the pueblo is not just a spatial device; it is a model of the ancient way of life.

N.Y. Pueblos were a result of selecting rational solutions under given circumstances, under the conditions that were extremely hard and allowed for minimal amount of freedom of choice. In Signal Camp, on the contrary, the rational and very compact assembly of functional units in the ravine landscape seems to be the driving force behind the spatial model for the Young Pioneers' camp, its structure, programme and concept. You can like the concept itself or you can dislike it. I, myself, always hated those camps, ever since I was a boy, but as I was designing the camp and working with the spatial component of its programme, I began feeling the unique nature of the idea behind the Young Pioneers' movement; maybe it was utopian

– and totalitarian, for many – but not without a sort of idealistic beauty.

O.Y. The 'building constructs' were among your very first projects. I can remember them very well. There, you had a series of schemes and constructions that were hard to miss. But later, with every project, your 'constructs' were more and more incorporated into something else. Is the architecture of movement flows part of your 'constructs', or is it a separate topic?

N.Y. I have inherited the architecture of movement flows from my father, who designed and built many transport hubs in his lifetime. There are a lot of passenger flow diagrams drawn by his hand. He was the source of this ideology of movement and flows, of the worship, I would even say, of flows of people. Many functionalists of his time worshiped this kind of thing. There is a theory of water flows, which studies how they behave if the speed difference between them is very big, or how they twirl or mix, what happens if a flow turns at a right angle. I think I have had the sense of those flows since I was a boy, the feeling that they simply have to be predetermined, although, in life, it is not necessarily true. I always aim at a geometric model of separating the flows, of doing things in a way where each turn would be smoothed over, or where there would be some sort of chamber to make the turn possible, where space would expand and turn, where there would be fewer staircases – ramps are better – so that one movement would gradually grow into another. I feel right-angled flow turns as a physical sensation of pain: it is as if a walking person has hit a wall. I love programs that model passenger flows, but I think that often it is a motivation for design rather than actual necessity. I do not like arbitrary drawing of pretty curves; there needs to be a meaningful geometry of turning nodes and the smoothness of a working mechanism based on movement.

Sometimes, the projection of flows ends up creating a streamlined, aerodynamically efficient bird-like shape. Our Olympic railway station in Sochi looks very much like a bird.[3] Its structure and shape are determined by the canopies above the railway tracks, while their shape is derived from movement

3 See page 207.
ARCHITECTS: Nikita Yawein, Vladimir Zenkevich, Vasily Romantsev, Zhanna Razumova, Pyotr Shlikhter, with Maria Vinogradova, Veronika Zhukova, Irina Kalinyakova, Evgenia Kuptsova, Ulyana Sulimova, Ksenia Schastlivtseva
STRUCTURAL ENGINEERS: Vladimir Gershtein, Dmitry Kresov, Rustem Akhimbekov, Andrey Krivonosov, Irina Lyashko, Natalia Prosvetova, Vladimir Turchevsky, Sergey Shvedov (Studio 44 Architects); Yury Bondarev, Dmitry Nikitin (LLC Tekton)
CHIEF ENGINEERS: Lev Gershtein, Vladimir Kremlyovsky

trajectories. Since the Olympic Park itself was organized along a radial scheme and the geometry of the railway tracks was also curved, the non-linear, bionic architecture of the railway station came about very naturally. We began with structuring the passenger flows and then went on to construct the whole train station complex as a living organism with a skeleton, the structural carcass of the building.

O.Y. This is how I have summed up your comments on your own projects: 'Functional requirements, regulations and constraints, movement diagrams, insolation diagrams, historic interpretations of the space, behavioural rituals – all of this and a lot more you combine in your mind to form force fields, functional, structural and spatial, and go on to work with the geometry of those fields as a single complex and conflicted phenomenon.' My résumé sounds overly highbrow and unintelligible. But can you ever explain things like that in a clear way?

N.Y. I will try. We have designed a lot of affordable housing and I have made my observations. Modifications in the shape of the building as its size increases, given the existing regulations, follow a certain logic. I even have diagrams of possible ways to expand the building without increasing apartment sizes – because if you are not limited by apartment size, anything is possible.

Let's take a look at an apartment building designed to comply to regulations on lighting, insolation, depth and size of rooms, and so on. Inside, there is a communication node: the greater the number of apartments it serves, the better. Such a centred house naturally grows into the shape of a star, a cross, a swastika or some such. If growth is inhibited on one side and the shape is 'squeezed', the growing star begins to twist. If such a building continues to grow, its centre becomes an empty space. If, at this point, the building keeps growing, the empty space grows to the point of becoming an atrium. The growth of this spatial organism is like a bubble: it grows, cracks and explodes.

The shape of any spatial organism experiences the impact of functional and spatial forces affecting it from the outside and from the inside.

The chaos of the external deforming forces can turn into the original pattern of the internal architectural order. The design of Boris Eifman Dance Academy began with tracing the contours of the complex shape formed by regulated distances from the neighbouring buildings.[4] It looks like a purely technical task for predesign site analysis. However, the original footprint area that strives to spread where possible, but is oppressed on all sides by intruding volumes, rights and needs of the surrounding buildings, already holds within itself a diagram of internal forces and external impacts. We used this diagram as the foundation for the rest of the design.

Cultural factors and interpretations, as well as historical memory, can also act as forces impacting the form. For example, in residential unit constructions, the diagram of the building in the form of a deep spatial niche is often used. The form is sort of already there, but, in those cases, I always ask myself, what is this? Where did it come from? It can be a cour d'honneur, coming from the French tradition of invitational space. Here, a lot is determined by the nature of the rituals you choose. On the other hand, the large spatial niche may be a reflection of the developer's requirements originating in Europe or the US, such as the requirement of providing a sea view to the greatest possible number of units and locations within the building. These are two prototypes for one scheme and two ways of modifying it under the influence of different forces, tensions and vectors. However, both radical differences and symbiotic solutions are possible in this case.

O.Y. You have spoken of form being influenced by functional and spatial forces, but suddenly tied them to historical prototypes. However, the modern architectural programme proclaimed 'planning without prototypes'. The form is not given; the form is a result. It is the constructivist 'ever unknown'. A good architectural solution is a discovery, and a project is a kind of invention. Whatever you say, this kind of thinking is an integral and inalienable part of your consciousness and of your work.

N.Y. Very possibly.

4 See page 251.
   ARCHITECTS: Nikita Yawein, Sergey Aksyonov, Marina Goryachkina, Valery Kulachenkov, Georgy Snezhkin, with Aleksey Vetkin
   STRUCTURAL ENGINEERS: Vladimir Gershtein, Irina Lyashko, Dmitry Kresov, Natalia Prosvetova, Elena Silantyeva

O.Y. At the same time, your architecture has always been filled with prototypes. Studio 44 Architects' projects would be well defined by a version of Voltaire's famous maxim: 'If prototypes did not exist, it would be necessary to invent them.' Even a seemingly confident new spatial or structural device looks as if it were still in search of its prototype, and, when it finds one, it begins its transformation, sometimes quite imperceptibly and sometimes very boldly.

N.Y. It is just that at some point an architectural solution acquires another dimension, which predetermines the direction for all further modifications, even geometric ones.

O.Y. You know, the point of the question is the nature of this 'other dimension'. In the work of Studio 44 Architects, prototypes are not 'archetypes', not Louis Kahn's 'forms', and not architectural quotes. They are very far from ambitious depth or historic truth; they refer to something tangible, imaginative, sometimes paradoxical, sometimes funny or amusing, but most often to something, if I may say so, 'unnecessary'. They are not examples accepted as basis, but rather a fragment of association fields that are generated during the design process. They do not so much contain the initial idea as a range of genetic and contextual links to something outside the project. But these selected links are introduced into the project as an internal driver of its development … The analogy is not to the prototype itself, but to its selected qualities, to its most prominent feature. Sometimes, it is just the link between a form and a name that invites various interpretations. Anyway, these features, characteristics and interpretations are then subject to various modifications.

N.Y. It depends. Sometimes there is just one prototype, and sometimes there are several. Some are fleeting – they emerge and dissolve during the design process – while others survive. Some exist in an unbreakable connection to each other, and some are completely independent. Some are intended to become the foundation of the design's structure, while others are distinctly meant to remain in the background. Prototypes do not have to be historical or architectural: they may come from nature, ship building, a child's toy – anything at all.

O.Y. Yes, but in all this diversity, it is possible to find figures, structures and architectural themes that become symbolic. They may be declared as a project's central concept, its dominant meaning. Their prototypes are proclaimed in the project's concept as succinct, symbolic graphic diagrams and drawings. Most often these graphical concepts turn up in competition projects. Is this worth believing or taking too literally? Or are they not the core imagery, but rather symbolic screens, behind which complex internal structures are hidden?

N.Y. Sometimes this is true, but there is no generic rule and you never know what the result will be. Every time, those things you call 'signs', 'symbols' or 'core images' are an inalienable part of the general concept. I have to point out that we never adapt the functional structure of the building to fit an image or a symbol. In our projects, we strive to achieve a natural symbiotic unity of imagery and function. Take the Palace of Schoolchildren in Astana.[5] The main symbol and motto of the project is the *shanyrak*, a round structure with an opening above the hearth that crowns a Kazakh yurt. In our project, the huge skylight above the atrium, which is the building's main public space, acts as the *shanyrak*. Both in the prototype, the yurt, and in the Palace of Schoolchildren the physics and metaphysics of the structural element are closely connected. The same is true for the Science and Technology Museum in Tomsk.[6] The towered wooden building stretches along the riverbank, and it really does resemble a fragment of the fortress that had been the starting point of the city. In this way, we revitalized the city's tradition of wooden architecture, and it does boast a great number of wonderful wooden buildings. These examples show that our imagery is not a screen, that it is not far-fetched.

O.Y. When you talk about 'architectural force fields', the spatial forces determining the geometry and architecture of a building include economic, sociocultural and other factors, both factual and theoretical. You said that a skyscraper is not a building, but a result of the interaction of forces …

---

5   See page 181.
   ARCHITECTS: Nikita Yawein, Sergey Aksyonov, Daria Gordina, Maryam Zamelova, Vladimir Zenkevich, Ivan Kozhin, Daria Nasonova, Natalia Poznyanskaya, Nikolay Smolin, Yanina Smolina, Georgy Snezhkin, with Natalia Arkhipova, Igor Britikov, Maria Vinogradova, Ilya Grigoryev, Nikita Zhukov, Veronica Zhukova, Evgenia Kuptsova, Elena Loginova, Nikolay Novotochinov, Ksenia Schastlivtseva, Anton Yar-Skryabin
   DESIGN AND WORKING DOCUMENTATION: developed in collaboration with LLC Bazis-Projekt LTD (Almaty)

6   See page 227.
   ARCHITECTS: Nikita Yawein, Anton Yar-Skryabin, with Alyona Amelkovich, Ivan Kozhin, Anna Kutilina, Roman Pokrovsky, Ksenia Schastlivtseva
   VISUALIZATION: Aleksey Vetkin, Andrey Patrikeyev

N.Y. Was that about the high-rise buildings by Ladozhsky railway station?[7] It was one of our most complex designs. It was never implemented because it was created right before a financial crisis. This project has to be viewed in the context of the time when everyone was hoping to build a skyscraper in the city centre. It was 'Asian skyscraping': a skyscraper was viewed as a symbol of prestige and power – the taller, the better – despite common sense or financial feasibility.

We placed our skyscrapers on the outskirts and made them not too tall; they could not be seen from the city centre. The important thing here is that we created not isolated skyscrapers, but a whole cluster of high-rise buildings that staked out the area with a new transport hub, very expensive land and very high rents.

The problem was that, in this spontaneous city core, there had already been some rather chaotic development: the streets crossed each other at irregular angles, and the building plots had very strange acute-angled shapes. The new railway station introduced additional complications. We were trying to find order in all of this – and it turned out that, if you connected the geometric centres of the plots, you ended up with a perfect pentagon, with Ladozhsky railway station at its base. So, we traced the plot contours so that they became as regularly shaped as possible and attempted to grow pyramidal 'crystals' out of them. On top, at the corners of our perfect district-forming pentagon, we placed perfect squares, triangles and pentagons, and made our way from the skyscrapers' top floors down to the point where the shapes above met the pyramids. Since the axes of the plots planned for sale did not completely coincide with the vertical axes of the perfect pentagon, the lower and middle sections of our skyscrapers were asymmetrical and tilted. Thus, chaos growing from below meets the order coming down from above. This geometry reflects the profitability curve: the most expensive real estate is on the lower levels, and the area of the lower levels is larger. Higher up, the rent gradually decreases, with the cheapest spaces located in the middle. From that point on, spaces, again, get more expensive: there are panoramic apartments.

So, first of all, it is not just one building, but a group of buildings. This strips the skyscraper of its sacred status right away and brings economic feasibility into the foreground. Secondly, the district is marked by a regular shape comprised of five vertical axes, and complete fuzziness of the layout below turns into order on top.

In this project, we attempted to provide an alternative to the somewhat manic desire, quite evident in the city, to make the skyscraper a magnificent building resembling Philip Johnson's New York high-rises: plinth, pillars, archways below and an elegant closing element on top. Everybody wants a classic three-part building stretched upwards …

Our proposal was a programmatic statement that a skyscraper is not a house and that the structure of a regular house is just not applicable. A skyscraper, first and foremost, is a product of economy; its growth is predetermined by external factors. All these influences yield an artificial shape – in this case, a crystal. All in all, by definition, the form of the skyscraper has nothing to do with any architectural form (ordered or modern).

O.Y. After the works of the Nobel laureate Ilya Prigogine, 'order out of chaos' is one of the star topics in world architecture. Many architectural concepts in the West relate to this idea, and a lot of critical works have been published in recent years. This theme has been interpreted in a variety of ways in various writings, but once it gets to actual architectural decision-making, it takes the form of turning or superimposing grids, 'fragmentation', deformation, deconstruction devices, and so on. And here you have a very complex approach not towards formal chaos, but to chaos in life. It is odd that you do not ascribe to any architectural or multidisciplinary ideology, even though you have read a lot of books on those subjects. Why is that?

N.Y. Well, first of all, I mostly speak to a different audience, and they do not really read this kind of literature. Secondly, what I find important is the complexity of architecture itself and the contradictory nature of impulses producing it. This real life, in itself, is far more interesting and meaningful than architectural and multidisciplinary theories and their philosophical speculations.

7   See page 265.
CONCEPT
ARCHITECTS: Nikita Yawein, Natalia Arkhipova, Vladimir Zenkevich, Yury Ashmetyev
HIGH-RISE BUILDING NO. 1
ARCHITECTS: Nikita Yawein, Nikolay Smolin, Yanina Smolina, Daria Nasonova, with Igor Britikov, Evgeny Korepanov, Natalia Poznyanskaya
STRUCTURAL ENGINEERS: Dmitry Kresov, Oleg Kurbatov, Irina Lyashko
MOCK-UP: Yakov Itsikson

O.Y. Then, my next question will concern this contradictory nature of initial impulses. In the difficult years after the revolution, a popular saying, typically ascribed to a rational European, preferably an Englishman, went, 'Russians love creating serious problems and then resolving them with difficulty.' In architecture, a similar thought – although not about the Russians – was voiced by Frank Lloyd Wright, who said, 'Limitations are no detriment to artist endeavor … Except as I were given some well defined limitations or requirements – the more specific the better – there would be no problem, nothing to work with, nothing to work out; why then trouble the artist?'[8]

You like exaggerating the programme's contradictions and placing yourself in a situation that rigidly dictates constraints and lack of freedom, a situation that provokes the search for a way out of a crisis through inventive devices. Often, the device comes as a first idea or a first hypothesis – and then, the way to resolve the problem reveals the problem itself. A different architectural reality proclaims itself, a reality where the logic of developing an independent version of resolving a problem lacks – or seems to lack – alternatives.

N.Y. When you find you've been 'cornered' – that's where everything starts … You have to be resourceful … This is where real architectural work begins. Here, professionalism really shows, as well as talent, by the way. It is not pure, clean-slate invention: you do not have to be an architect to come up with pretty compositions given complete freedom; or, at least, you do not have to be too familiar with the difficulties, 'the underbelly' of our profession. But when the plot you get is small and dark and squeezed on all sides by the surrounding buildings, and the regulations are extremely limiting … Boris Eifman Dance Academy recently received a World Architecture Festival Award in the schools category. The initial design challenge behind this 'temple of art' had nothing to do with composition or architecture as art. The allocated plot was too tight to fit all of the required spaces. Many thought that it would be impossible to do that without creating tiny rooms and rooms with no natural light.

As a result of the long design process, in the new building, functional volumes take up all the existing space, with practically no space left over. From outside inwards and from inside outwards, there grows a complex structure of various functional blocks with twelve dance halls. In the very heart of the building, at different levels, a narrow 'gap' takes up the whole height of the building: it is a top-lit lounge space.

Thus, from the multitude of factors hindering the building process, through resolving a multitude of challenges, a very special space of light appeared: something we have never done before and never tried to replicate since. In this building, the glass façades of the dance halls look out not only on the outside, but also on the inside. This allowed us to direct extra light to the different levels and into the centre of the lounge space. The architecture of the building predetermines two moods: in the single lounge space, it is play, noise, running up and down stairs; in the isolated dance rooms behind matt glass, it is concentration, aloofness, energy and discipline, hard work. From the lounges, the matt glass creates the impression of a shadow theatre. The life of the building develops at the edge of these two mood states.

The dance rooms with translucent glass walls facing the street and matt glass walls facing the inside of the building act as light-carrying locks between the outer world and the narrow and deep core of vertically connected lounge spaces. With the lights turned on, the shadows and silhouettes of dancers practising become sharper …

The dance rooms have an atmosphere of an aquarium filled with coloured air. It is the special ballet space, the space of flight, leaps and supports. I think people like to dive into this atmosphere. Such effects are impossible to predict. There is a feeling of lightness, almost of weightlessness. You lose the sensation of what is up and what is down. Each dance room has windows and a translucent wall, two walls of matt glass, different textures of white, mirror surface with dancers' reflections, brightly coloured floors. The coloured floors and white textures are reflected and deflected in the glass. In this 'weighted' colour environment, the eye relaxes and rests. In addition, the air becomes movable and coloured, because

---

8   Frank Lloyd Wright, *The Future of Architecture*, New York, 1953, p. 94.

the scattered light is reflected in different ways. Lounge spaces are only two-thirds of their usual size, but they look as if they were several times larger.

O.Y. You said, 'When you find you've been "cornered" – that's where everything starts.' This is true … But who corners whom?! I think you have always liked to 'corner' yourself, as you call it, into situations where it seemed impossible not only to reconcile contradictory interests, but also to fit in the required spaces. I can't help thinking that the search for an architectural solution in cases like these has recently become, for you, something like a way of making all the other parties of the design process play by your rules. Before, architects used to inspire clients and governments by architectural ideas that could change the world. Now, no one is going to sacrifice anything for ideas, and no one is going to understand serious professional concepts. You told me yourself that you do not take up projects for private villas because there are no clients who both have the money and are willing to organize their lives along architectural principles. But the city centre has plenty of development cases that are impossible to resolve without damaging the historic urban fabric. And it's in situations like these that you can quickly show 'who is boss', can prove that things have to be done the right and the only way…

N.Y. Right: for private houses, we do not yet have clients with a truly deep understanding of architecture. Or we have not educated them.

But the story of the dance academy contradicts everything you have just said … Everyone told me that Maestro Eifman is impossible to work with, that he is unbearable, that he does not like anything at all. My experience was just the opposite: yes, Boris Eifman has his own unique opinion on everything, but he is a man of exquisite artistic culture, and I found working with him interesting and exciting. I think of him as my rightful co-author.

Coming back to the point of your question, you are quite right. Complex, contradictory, unfavourable situations are, for me, a means of 'making architecture'. But that is not the main point. Sometimes, we get projects where the initial

contradictions between all sorts of regulations and stakeholder interests had already been left unresolved by another architect. They are very difficult. They require numerous repeat approvals; sometimes, we have to introduce drastic changes to the project, and such projects are almost never profitable. So, it's not so simple; you have to pay for your pleasure …

O.Y. You have switched to the complex and contradictory nature of restoration and reconstruction within protected historic areas, in the proximity of historical monuments and even within the historical monuments. But such projects are your credo and your forte.

N.Y. In my first reconstruction projects, I realized that the most important thing in this work is finding the boundary between the acceptable and the unacceptable. It is very thin and vague, but it's important not just to understand it, but also to feel its presence, to acknowledge its presence along the regulations and guidelines that you need to follow anyway. The work is very interesting, and you end up creating something significant when the architectural solution you have found is an embodiment of some limit, overstepping which – whether in terms of dimensions, plasticity and style, or height – brings about the collapse of the integrity of the old and the new, the destruction of contextual links. Sometimes, the result is just limp: you have not violated anything, but neither have you created anything good. In this case, the quality of the urban fabric degrades; it becomes less viable, less attractive and less valuable. It is too loose – and, sooner or later, the historic environment suffers from blunt intrusions. When you design for a historic centre, you not only have to preserve it, you also need to 'keep up the quality'. It is important to find the critical point, to feel the internal trigger that gives life to the environment and the situation, to determine the amount and nature of acceptable change. Be it dimensions, materials, type or amount of intervention, there is a limit beyond which you simply cannot go, but it lures you to approach as close as possible. Every historic context has its own unique balance. It is important to find yourself 'on the edge', but to prevent movement beyond it; to climb to the very top without falling down the precipice.

O.Y. 'On the edge …' But many, if not everybody, will not understand what you mean. What is this invisible line, and why is it exactly where you say it is?

N.Y. Many – a lot of people – do understand, or you can explain it to them. In the mid-1990s, we were working on the atrium at Nevsky 25, our first big reconstruction project in the centre of St Petersburg.[9] It was then that, partly due to some external circumstances, we faced the challenge of designing on the edge of what was possible. Afterwards, also because of my work on the preservation of cultural monuments, I spent a lot of time trying to understand and to explain to others what those boundaries beyond which the fabric of culture and history fell apart were. We did this in many projects, with different contexts and in different ways. The theoretical moves were explored and described in actual projects. It is not only about intuition, but also largely about the knowledge, the overall understanding of culture – and that is something you can work on.

O.Y. You often turn to Russian architecture before Peter the Great. What do you find most interesting there? Is it the 'ties of time' or the impulses for new constructs?

N.Y. Both. Byzantine architecture gave us a hierarchy of images and things. It is one of the foundations of Russian architecture; a Westerner does not understand it. Take a small church in a small town, a church in a town slightly bigger, and an enormous cathedral in the capital city! They are like nesting dolls: they are all similar, although different. In Russia, houses and churches are assembled from houses, churches, logs, blocks and autonomous parts. You can identify combinations of some initial elements: anteroom, ground floor, house. There is a notion of 'cell structure', where a house is made of houses just like it; however, I have never seen a detailed historic and architectural description of this system.

In settlements and buildings, scale and importance increase closer to the centre. The pyramidal centricity may be turned out onto a plane. In our project for the Solovki settlement, centred symmetry is turned out onto a plane and presented as a panoramic picture.[10] You can find such panoramas in the surviving villages of the Russian north: small bath houses in the front, barns behind them, houses behind the barns, and the main church behind them all: the larger the building, the further away it is. It is like the reverse perspective of medieval icons.

Exploring several versions of a theme in one building is very typical for Russian architecture. Thus, turrets of fortresses and monasteries are often all different, of every possible shape: circle, square, octagon, hexagon, etc. Each version may yield its own plasticity development of parts and details. I think it is a very good modern principle, so we began using it a lot.

O.Y. The notion of genius loci implies addressing some basic memories, substances, developmental triggers lying below the surface, beyond external similarities and familiar forms. There are few architectural tasks where the direct approach towards the goal leads astray and success results from a series of accidents. However, with Studio 44 projects, this is very often pointed out.

N.Y. Genius loci as an implied idea is part of a lot of projects done by Studio 44 Architects. However, as a goal and a dominant element of the whole concept, it was implemented in the projects for the Solovetsky Islands, in the General Staff Building of the State Hermitage, the project for the reconstruction of St Petersburg's city centre, in the project for one of the seaside districts of St Petersburg, and in the reconstruction of the historical centre of Kaliningrad. In all of these projects, the notion of genius loci takes on the primary role. I will tell you about some of them.

Vladimir Lemekhov and I did a project that did not go further than a sketch, but, for us, it was very important. In the vicinity of St Petersburg, on the Gulf of Finland, there is a large bay that appeared very recently on the spot from which sand for the construction of the dam and other protection facilities was loaded onto barges. We designed a large city-on-the-water district, where we developed an extensive typology of St Petersburg housing – the kind of housing that had never been built anywhere in St Petersburg, but which should have

---

9 ARCHITECTS: Nikita Yawein, Sergey Sokolov, Vitaly Antipin, Pavel Sokolov, Eduard Tyshersky

10 See page 59.
ARCHITECTS: Nikita Yawein, Svetlana Borisenkova, Vitaly Antipin, with Olga Igonina, Margarita Yawein
STRUCTURAL ENGINEER: Leonid Kaplan

emerged if the initial concept of the city itself had been taken through to its logical end.[11]

They call St Petersburg the 'Venice of the North'. It was probably like that in the times of Peter the Great, but, since then, St Petersburg has never resembled even Amsterdam. The significance of water-based communication systems kept diminishing, and the canals were fewer and fewer in number. In the reign of Peter the Great, every city resident was officially required to have a boat; now, the few yacht owners have nowhere to dock them. We created a typology of canals, ranging from small and narrow to long and wide, and a gradual system of transforming them into bodies of water with islands, and islands with bodies of water. At some points, the relationship between land and water was turned inside out.

Then, we tried adding a typology of waterside housing to the typology of bodies of water: villas on private islands, small private cottages, semi-detached houses with front yards, apartment blocks, and residential complexes with developed infrastructures and services. Each building, whether a villa or an apartment building, could be approached by boat and by car. It was a project for a specific city district, but at the same time it was a model of Peter the Great's unfulfilled dreams.

We have won two large-scale competitions for city-centre reconstructions, in St Petersburg[12] and in Kaliningrad.[13] In both projects, we were looking for models of human life that would meet the residents' expectations. Both projects are a search for what had been lost: in Kaliningrad, it was loss through destruction; in St Petersburg, it was loss through dilapidation, both material and spiritual.

You know, I think I would say that our projects in Astana were also a search for genius loci. Astana is a very young city. Kisho Kurokawa, who developed its master plan, designed it as a city of primary geometric shapes. I love Astana for being a city that has not yet passed through the filters of history and has not yet developed constraints that are so typical of old capital cities. It is a training ground for bold experimentation with primary shapes. However, there is an ancient civilization with a unique cultural tradition behind this new capital city, and it is looking to create ties with it. It is a city in search of the genius loci.

In the Palace of Schoolchildren in Astana, we made the top part of the building in the shape of a disc, with the steppe horizon on the roof … The planetarium rises above it like a mound, and below all of that are huge glass volumes, each with its own traditional ornament.

O.Y. We keep talking about space. Maybe it is time to move on to something more material and simple. You always liked to talk about brick …

N.Y. Brickwork architecture has been playing a large role in our latest project. I think, today, brick is not a constructional material. Earlier, the architecture of a building was determined not by brick itself, but by brick structures: there were brickwork archways, vaults, walls. For me, the nature of brick is most fully and strongly represented in the architecture of Byzantium and Persia. I always found it odd, unnatural even, when I saw brickwork forms that were not inherently brickwork, for example, ancient orders. Today, on large brick surfaces, brick is always a filling, and the combinations of bricks are not structural elements anymore. Brickwork can be used to create something like pixel compositions with a great potential for the decorative and spontaneous. Actually, I saw something like that in medieval Persian buildings. Brickwork architecture there is magnificent: it is very structured, but, at the same time, brickwork seems to be playing with itself at all times, seemingly forgetting all about structural systems.

Our firm has designed buildings with five or six different types of brick texture. Modern carpet neogeometric ornaments appear as pixel improvisations. For the residential building on Petrograd Side, we used a whole library of different stone textures and types of brickwork, having included sculptured reliefs as parts of the wall.[14] The components of this collection date back to the early twentieth century, but, as a whole, it is mixed and scattered in a new, seemingly arbitrary order. Sometimes the whole wall is covered with different brickwork textures as if they were paintings, but the image that I personally find important here is that of an antiques shop. The accidental and yet comprehensive set of items in an antiques shop reflects the culture a lot fuller than an art gallery, does it not?

11 See page 273.
   ARCHITECTS: Nikita Yawein, Vladimir Lemekhov

12 See page 295.
   ARCHITECTS: Nikita Yawein, Oleg Yawein, Maria Vinogradova, Ilya Grigoryev, Ivan Kozhin, Vladimir Lemekhov, Andrey Patrikeyev, Georgy Snezhkin
   PROJECT ANNOTATION: Lyudmila Likhacheva

13 See page 301.
   ARCHITECTS: Nikita Yawein, Ilya Grigoryev, Ivan Kozhin, Ksenia Schastlivtseva
   VISUALIZATION: Aleksey Vetkin, Andrey Patrikeyev
   PROJECT ANNOTATION: Lyudmila Likhacheva
   TRAFFIC: Gennady Shelukhin (Territorial Development Institute)

14 ARCHITECTS: Nikita Yawein, Ivan Kozhin, Julia Dubeiko, Vadim Ponomaryov
   STRUCTURAL ENGINEERS: Vladimir Ioffe, Dmitry Kresov, Elena Silantyeva

The library or antiques shop of brickwork and texture is just one layer of wall architecture, which also includes a 'library' of openings, windows, glass panes, balconies, railings, and so on. At the same time, as in art nouveau, windows of different sizes and shapes can be categorized as openings for the eye and for the light. As a result, apartment layouts are projected outwards and join our pixel ornaments. The structure of the wall maintains its ties with the St Petersburg tradition and the style of the surrounding buildings, but it is also transformed. Garrets, for example, used to be cheap built-on lodgings moved somewhat deeper inside the building above the cornice. In the times of elevators, the top floor is the most expensive space in a building. We showed that by sloping the wall inwards instead of making a backward step above the cornice.

O.Y. But this is something you do not only to the wall, but also to the whole structure of a façade or building. The first courtyard façades of the bank on Furshtatskaya Street display a range of typical St Petersburg forms: granite embankments, colonnades, railings, crowns, roofs.[15] Isn't it the same principle that you used in City on the Water? There, you employed every possible way to tie in land, water and buildings – and the resulting types of buildings, canals, havens and islands. You are taking inventory, archiving things – and then you create a new hierarchy and montage. By the way, is this in any way connected to the various fragmentation devices that have such a long tradition in the art and architecture of the twentieth and twenty-first centuries?

N.Y. Fragmentation is more about theory and critique. For me, the important thing is quite different: along with the design commission we get from the client and the requirements from the authorities, there is one more set of specifications, the one that I, as an architect, do for myself. This design brief, the one of my own, is derived from what 'the project wants'.

O.Y. So, the entity that 'wants' in this case is not a building, a structure or a material, the way Louis Kahn had it, but the project itself, a future and as yet unfound architectural solution?

N.Y. I am talking about a different thing – about my personal design brief and specifications, which are based on the understanding of the interests that prevail and inspire a given project: its function; the client, or my idea of the client; some features of the site or its history; the surroundings; the mythology behind the building, the location or the surroundings … It can be the current issues in architectural politics. For instance, another project could have failed approval; there could have been a conflict between the authorities and the client or between the architect's design and the general public. Then, in my mind – sometimes it is conscious and sometimes it is not – I go through all the ways undertaken to solve similar problems in the past. I take them out, develop them, invent a more powerful response to the challenges. This is the way the main project vector develops, along with a number of sidelines, which are also important to remember in your work, to bring up to date and in line with the overall project. Then, the architectural devices that have a parallel life in your mind and memory begin to acquire a structure suitable to the project: they form a certain hierarchy; you finalize them and alter them, sometimes to the point where it becomes unrecognizable. At times, a half-forgotten theme suddenly springs up and becomes the main one. So, it is important to remember the half-forgotten themes, the ideas you have cast away, and fleeting impressions.

The most curious thing is that, as you work on a project, it transforms you as much as you transform it. When I say things like 'the point of view of the project', 'interests of the project', 'desires of the project', they are not metaphors. The project truly does have a will of its own, which makes you change, activate or subdue whole areas of your architectural consciousness. For this very reason, I like to change up the types of architectural tasks: locations, functions and scale range from huge master plans to small reconstruction projects. It is the accidental or peripheral themes that sometimes create a developmental explosion when they are moved to the head of the project. And the themes that have remained central for a long time invariably become too formal and lifeless.

15 See page 83.
ARCHITECTS: Nikita Yawein, Nina Balazh, with Vladimir Zenkevich, Vladimir Parfyonov
STRUCTURAL ENGINEER: Veniamin Kuper

O.Y. Since you've mentioned the brief that an architect develops for himself, I feel that I can now talk to you about something I have long wanted to discuss. Studio 44 Architects has done a number of urban-development projects where the architectural component is a design brief, a programme identifying acceptable parameters and methods for an architect's work. I think this genre calls for a commentary.

N.Y. This kind of work originated from developing new project programmes of our own. We did this together with our clients, or at our clients' request, and offered our programme ideas. We developed the building programme for the Palace of Schoolchildren in Kazakhstan. And when we were developing the programme for our other project in Astana, Zhastar Youth Palace, it was as if we were already planning the project itself.[16] We specified what the client was apparently hoping for – a conglomeration of a variety of functions, each of them seemingly uninteresting on its own, but very interesting as a single whole. We immediately envisioned this collection of functions as a bubble or a ball where everything was crammed together. It is an intrinsically non-hierarchical system, a conglomeration, but at the same time it is an oecumene of sorts. Later, as we were working on the actual project, the bubble turned into a cube.

Apparently, any more or less comprehensive programme presupposes an appropriate spatial equivalent of some sort. So, we started inventing programmes derived from the spatial models we had discovered and offering them to clients. Now I think that it is generally impossible to develop a comprehensive programme if you do not have a spatial model in mind, even a very rough one, even subconsciously. Our submission for Zhastar Youth Palace was, in fact, an embodiment of such a presupposed model: it was a design programme packed in specific geometric forms in a certain way.

O.Y. But how do such models comply with the current regulations?

N.Y. I always found designing urban districts rather odd because the system of existing regulations and guidelines always predetermines their structure: streets and buildings along the perimeter, schools and kindergartens in the middle, and so on. It is an intellectualized, made-up system that has its roots in the rigorous planning of life in the 1960s. We made an attempt at understanding how we could make the city we wanted within the existing regulatory framework. At the crossroads between the available and the desired, solutions can be found, and sometimes there is the only possible way to do things, from the size of the city block or width of a driveway to the arrangement of residential units. We tried to find urban-development solutions that would also work as an architectural brief for the buildings that would be making up the city we wanted to see. But the most important thing was that such a brief was, in fact, a brief to create a good building. We realized that a good building can only result from a good brief that is a product of a good urban environment.

O.Y. Are you saying that every idea of a perfect city triggers a typology of good buildings?

N.Y. In recent years, projects have been successful only if they had a persuasive scenario behind them. When you are working on a building in a dense historic environment, you follow the rules of the game and the memories that spring from this environment. Outside of the historic environment, the rules of the game generally become vague and artificial. For me, urban development is finding and developing the rules for designing specific and different buildings.

O.Y. However, in the development concepts for the historic centres of St Petersburg and Kaliningrad, as well as in the project for the Centre of Modern Culture at New Holland, it seems that Studio 44 Architects programmatically avoids the architectural design of specific beautiful and different buildings. In the project for Kaliningrad, building design was assigned to students, as if you were offering it to just anyone to design good buildings along the given rules of the game. So, your architecture is your programme.

16 See page 193.
    ARCHITECTS: Nikita Yawein, Daria Gordina, Vladimir Lemekhov, Vasily Romantsev, Anna Rudenko, Georgy Snezhkin, Maria Spivak, Ulyana Sulimova
    STRUCTURAL ENGINEER: Yury Bondarev (Tekton LLC)
    CHIEF ENGINEER: Lev Gershtein
    DESIGN AND WORKING DOCUMENTATION: developed in collaboration with LLC Bazis-Projekt LTD (Almaty)

N.Y. In urban-development projects, we transfer the experience of programme development that I described in Kazakhstan onto a new scale. These projects are spatial life scenarios. Our project for Kaliningrad is a model of a historic pedestrianized city with a great number of small business owners and a set of services and functions typical for such a life. The Königsberg of old initially had many parts with very different spatial structures that, at the same time, functioned along the same principle: small-sized ownerships, maximum density, and a great diversity of links. As we were working on the project, it became obvious that both the parameters of the buildings and their history are perfectly consistent with the model we had assumed. The project is aimed at preserving everything that is genuine, and at finding everything that has a timeless value.

The project for the reconstruction of St Petersburg's city center was largely triggered by the romantic atmosphere of communicating courtyards. Historically, city blocks in St Petersburg replaced large noble estates, so they tend to be several times bigger than regular city blocks and their shapes are very diverse. We arrived at an ideal model of a city interconnected by a system of passages through the courtyards incorporating public functions. One could say that, in this project, a romantic notion produced functionalism.

For everyone, New Holland is a very large old building for drying wood or a group of buildings that could be brought together in a single complex. We made New Holland a small city or a model of a city with a great number of small blocks with functions of their own. The blocks are permanent, while their functions may alter.

O.Y. For me, the idea of spatial models of life is related to the attempts of modern science in spatial modelling for non-spatial phenomena and notions. In human culture, social, political, moral and other ideas invariably acquire spatial characteristics. This is evident in ancient religious architecture and in the architecture of symbolism and the avant-garde. If we go back to the beginning of this interview, there appears a chain of thought of growing complexity: building constructs; models of movement in architectural form; 'architectural force fields', where economic, social and cultural factors are among the forces that determine the geometry and architecture of the building; models of architectural order growing out of chaos; and, finally, spatial models of life. All of this is very inspirational. However, there is one question: to what degree is the idea of spatial models acting as the foundation for a project a renewed version of the utopian, personal and other models that had been so persistently incorporated in everyday life in the period of the avant-garde?

N.Y. Without a spatial model of life, there is no architecture. The question is, where does everything come from and what form does it take on? I have already said that, if there is regulatory documentation, there must be a presupposed spatial model. And why would a way of thinking originating from a spatial model be less viable than a way of thinking coming from a regulation or any other text? We develop spatial parameters of a life already in place; we do not invent models people should follow in their lives. I am not at all interested in the latter kind of models. I want to understand what life is really like and what the right vessel is to hold it.

O.Y. I have not asked you about specific projects, but there is one I cannot help asking you about. I have said and written a great deal about our work for the Hermitage extension in the East Wing of the General Staff Building.[17] I think our readers would like to know your views on that project.

N.Y. What I find most important about that project is the street space within the building: a large urban space surrounded by a sea of small rooms, hallways and staircases. In that building, even in an isolated small room, you cannot help being included in the enormity of which the small room is a part. This is what makes the new spatial structure of the General Staff Building so intense. It is especially diverse and powerful in the labyrinths of the top floor: there are many rooms without skylights, but with views over the city, as well as domes, as well as concrete skylight pyramids, as well as bridge walkways at an enormous height, as well as dark halls

17 See page 149.
   ARCHITECTS: Oleg Yawein, Nikita Yawein, Vladimir Lemekhov, Pavel Sokolov, with Vitaly Antipin, Irina Golysheva, Sergey Dryazzhin, Evgeny Elovkov, Veronika Zhukova, Irina Krylova, Vladimir Parfyonov, Georgy Snezhkin, Sergey Sologub, Varvara Khmelyova, Anton Yar-Skryabin
   RESTORATION: Grigory Mikhailov (Mikhailov Architectural Studio); Oleg Kuzevanov, Natalia Shirokova (Studio 44 Architects)
   STRUCTURAL ENGINEERS: Vladimir Ioffe, Dmitry Kresov, Oleg Kurbatov, Irina Lyashko, Dmitry Yaroshevsky

above the archways … Unfortunately, these spaces are still isolated or closed, but sooner or later the single museum space on the top floor of the General Staff Building will emerge. The continuity and openness of routes, especially the continuity of circular routes with panoramic views of the city, is very important here. The panoramic views are a typological feature of the Hermitage: this is much spoken of, and the Winter Palace is famous for them. However, even in the Winter Palace they are not continuous, and museum routes digress from the outer contour of the building. Continuous circular routes looking over Palace Square and the Moika Embankment, and on three levels, appeared only now, in the General Staff Building.

O.Y. I want to try tying together everything you have said in a simple list of conversation topics. So, you spoke about designing as constructing, about architectural force fields, about analogues and parallels in architectural structures from different times and cultures, about prototypes and genius loci, about the new tectonics of the brick wall, and about some other topics. It is a very fragmented and incomplete list, but it demonstrates a consistent view of architecture and a design system. It is something that many people notice, as I said at the very beginning of our interview. Why do you talk so little about all of this when you work? And do not tell me that you do not think about any of this when you are working.

N.Y. I spoke about the things you were asking about, about the backstage processes of my architectural work. They are, of course, important for me, but I am not sure that I can impose this on the architects with whom I work or on my clients. And, of course, this is nothing to be turned into an architectural credo for the firm. An architectural solution must speak for itself. A project can be explained in many ways. Different architects and clients may find very different arguments persuasive. As for the fact that my observations and feelings form a sort of system, as you say, well, you are a better judge of that. For me, it is best not to know about it, or, at least, not to think about it too much – or I might find myself influenced by

my own theory. And I have no time for that … Over 150 people are working at Studio 44 Architects at the moment. You cannot create architecture through dispensing orders; you need a dialogue, clear heads, arguments, discussions and peer-to-peer sharing when ideas and proposals speak for themselves, no matter who made them. You have to know how to lead your group in such a context and how to avoid losing your own way while working like that.

WORKS

What follows is a cross-section of a much larger number of projects and buildings designed by Nikita Yawein and Studio 44 since the 1980s. The selection shows the consistency of an architectural approach that is based not on a specific style or signature, but on a rigorous conceptual attitude towards architecture, buildings and the city.

The selected projects are grouped in thematic chapters, whose sequence more or less follows the chronology of the oeuvre. This allows for a double reading of the work, tracing the evolution and the increase in scale and complexity of the projects, and revealing how forms and ideas have been unfolding and maturing over time.

Hans Ibelings

EARLY WORKS

The earliest work of Nikita Yawein was made before he had
started, and actually *could* have started, Studio 44, which,
as a private practice, became possible only after the end of
communism. These works reveal a rigorous and principled
approach, with elementary geometry as their point of departure.
Aside from a skilful hand and a great spatial imagination, the
projects demonstrate how much freedom is offered by self-
imposed limitations of geometrical configuration. In some ways
the geometry can be understood as a tool for bypassing and
overcoming the constraints of the Soviet building industry,
which, especially in the area of housing, was geared towards
an extremely efficient, if not frugal, standardization. In the
Cube Residential Estate, the use of a system of prefab walls
and columns – with a Miesian section – allows the project to
adhere to the economic and societal realities of the time while
simultaneously offering an alternative.

The same pragmatic idealism lies behind A Home for Three
Generations of One Family, which balances a desire to preserve
the Uzbek tradition of living in multi-generational households
with the realities of contemporary large-scale housing, again
based on an elementary geometry.

While in these two projects geometry was the point of
departure, in the Pioneer camp and the Amphitheatre of Boxes,
it was also its conclusion. Here, the geometry creates patterns
of repeated forms, which are structured by means of symmetry.
In different guises, the theme of geometry, as explored in these
early works, would become a structuring tool for nearly every
work by Studio 44.

Hans Ibelings

01

THE CUBE RESIDENTIAL ESTATE

In the Cube Residential Estate, a competition design, apartment buildings are constructed from cubic modules measuring $3 \times 3 \times 3$ m. One unit of living space (one 'cube') can be used for different purposes, such as a hall and toilet, a kitchen, a bedroom, a living room or an office. The basic unit of space can be increased; a bedroom for a couple with a baby, for example, would occupy two cubes.

The design features apartments that range in size from 32.5 to 119 sq m, for families numbering from one to ten people. Common to all the apartments – the hub around which all the other rooms are configured – is a block of 3.5 cubes comprising the kitchen, living room and dining room, with upper side lighting. Raising the ceiling by half a level highlights the central common area in the single-level apartments. Adjacent to the kitchen/dining areas are square, open-air terraces.

The apartments are grouped around stairwells (6×3 m in plan), forming a building of three or four storeys. Different arrangements of apartment blocks form a dense construction fabric, with closed-off inner courtyards and passageways running between the rows of buildings. The 'Anthill' version of the design, a picturesque mountain of cubes, captures the very essence of this architectural approach.

CLIENT: N/A
DESIGN: 1976 (competition design)
REALIZATION: N/A
TOTAL AREA: N/A

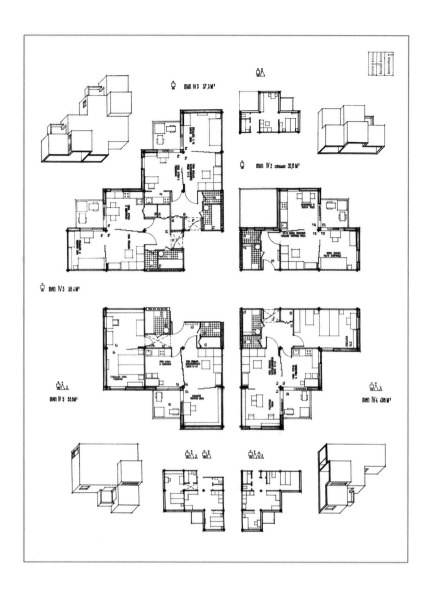

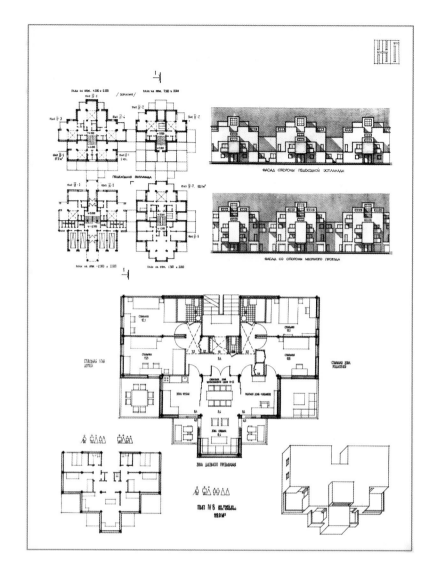

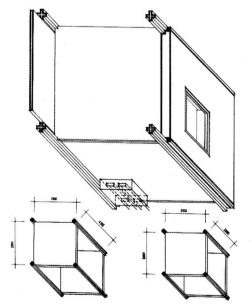

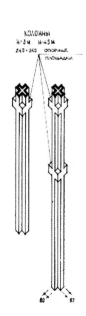

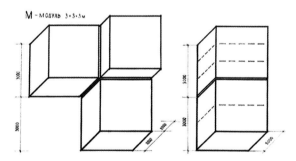

ABOVE, TOP
Designs for apartments for families of up to five people (left) and for three generations of one family (seven to nine people; right).

ABOVE
Axonometric projection showing the interlocking of multiple cubes.

LEFT
The basic construction elements of each cube.

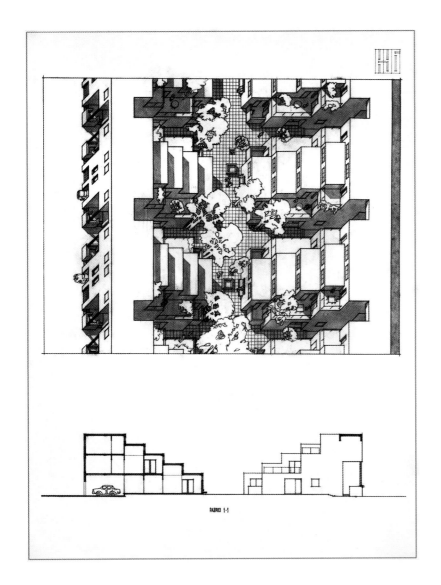

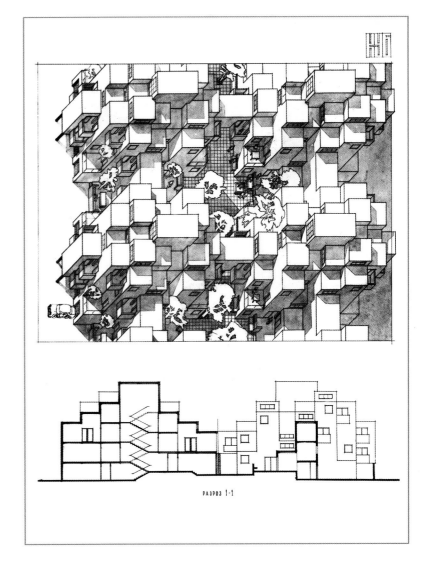

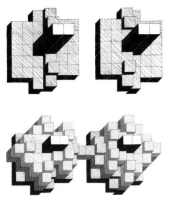

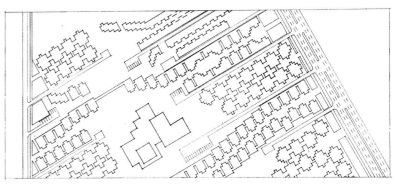

Axonometric projection and cross-section of the terrace-style layout of apartments.

Axonometric projection and cross-section of the 'Anthill' layout.

Diagram showing the sequence of construction using the cubic modules.

Draft outline of the residential estate, showing the different arrangements of apartment building.

02

A HOME FOR THREE GENERATIONS OF ONE FAMILY

This project, an apartment building, looks at ways in which architecture might be used to preserve and cultivate traditional Uzbek family life. Each unit of housing in the building is intended to accommodate three generations of the same family (six to seven people), spread over three and a half levels. The lower level is designed for the older generation, the upper levels for their children and grandchildren. The kitchen-diner is located on the second level. From here it is half a level up to the high-ceilinged (4.2 m), spacious (5 × 5 m) living room. The upper level has a ceiling height of 2.7 m and contains the bedrooms for the younger generations.

The units are built in sets of two, separated by an open-air section two storeys high – a garden located on the older generation's level. The garden is shared by the two units and, if desired, can be divided in half by a hedge. The forerunner of this type of recreation area in Central Asian architecture was the *iwan*, a terrace or gallery with a flat ceiling supported by columns or posts. However, unlike the *iwan*, which was walled on three sides, air passes through this system of terraces, a great advantage in the sultry Tashkent summers. The narrow strips of ribbon windows on the south-facing façades are another nod to the hot climate.

The accessible part of the building's roof is fenced off with high walls, creating a shared garden for all residents. In this way, the project combines the benefits of urban development with the age-old desire to live in harmony with nature. Like everything in the East, the structure of the building follows a specific hierarchy: the bedrooms form an amphitheatre around the living room, the apartments a similar one around the *iwan*-inspired garden.

Tashkent, Uzbekistan

CLIENT: N/A
DESIGN: 1978 (competition design)
REALIZATION: N/A
TOTAL AREA: N/A

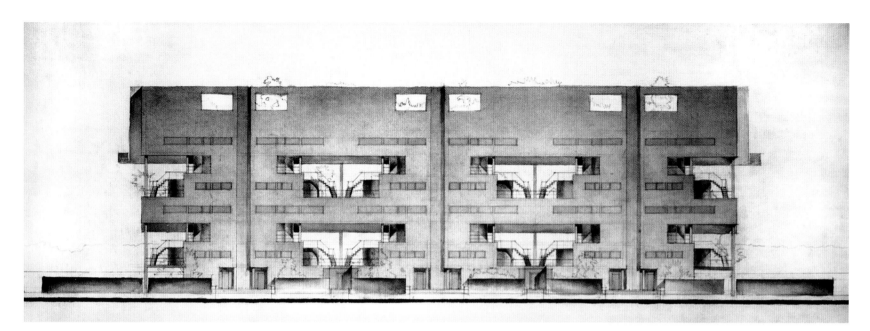

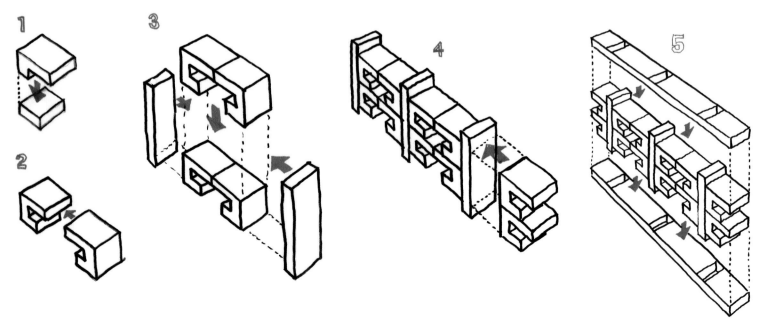

OPPOSITE, TOP
Sketch of the south-facing façade.

OPPOSITE, CENTRE
Sketch of the north-facing façade.

OPPOSITE, BOTTOM
Sequence showing how the basic elements of the design are combined to form an apartment building.

RIGHT
From top: lower-level floor plan showing the living space for the elderly and garden; second-level floor plan showing the kitchen-diner and terraces; upper-level floor plan showing the dining room and beds for the middle and youngest generations.

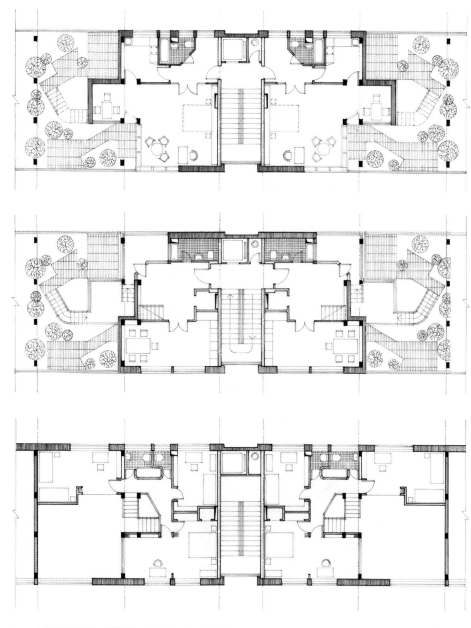

RIGHT
A model of the apartment building, viewed from the south.

03

SIGNAL CHILDREN'S PIONEER CAMP

Each accommodation unit at Signal Children's Pioneer Camp is designed to house four schoolchildren of the same age. A block comprising a row of seven units can house a group of twenty-eight children, known as a troop. The camp is large enough to accept twelve troops at a time, in six different age groups, from eleven to sixteen. The rows of accommodation cascade down the sides of a cliff, with the rooms for the oldest children at the top, and those for the youngest at the bottom. The accessible roof areas of the buildings serve as outdoor terraces for the levels above them. The tiers are connected by steps, and two areas of each tier serve as open-air circulation spaces.

The accommodation units are at a 45-degree angle to the corridors, facing the sea. This ensures that the units are well ventilated throughout. The zigzag pattern, with interlocking units, gives the camp structural stability in an area of the Caucasian foothills known for its seismic activity.

The central axis of the camp follows the bottom of a ravine, while the streams that run down to the sea fill a series of decorative pools. At the top, the axis runs through a four-storey building containing offices, a canteen and a club. At the bottom, there is an amphitheatre and a circular arena for parades, campfires and other Young Pioneer rituals. In fact, the whole complex, with its system of viewing terraces, is nothing short of a huge amphitheatre in a sea-and-cliff setting, its residents alternating between actors and audience.

Caucasus, Black Sea Region, Russia

CLIENT: N/A
DESIGN: 1985
REALIZATION: N/A
TOTAL AREA: N/A

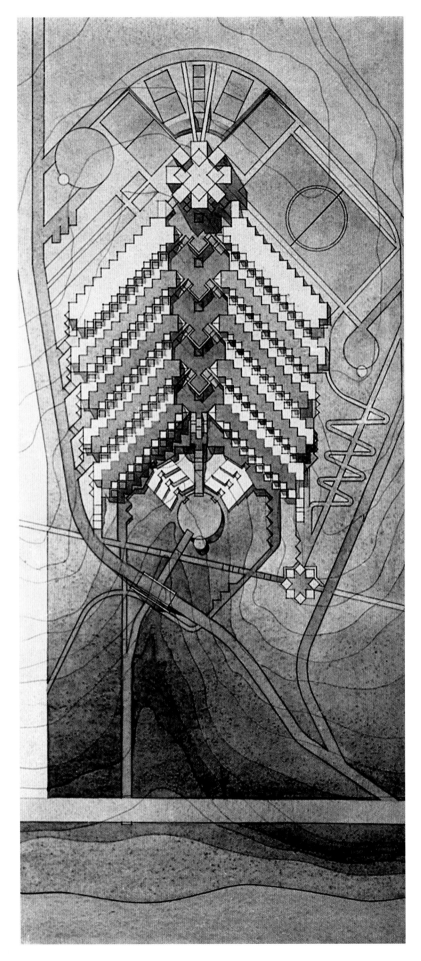

LEFT
Sketch showing the topography
of the site.

ABOVE
Detail of sample floor plan.

OPPOSITE, TOP
The mock-up of the camp.

OPPOSITE, BOTTOM
Longitudinal cross-section.

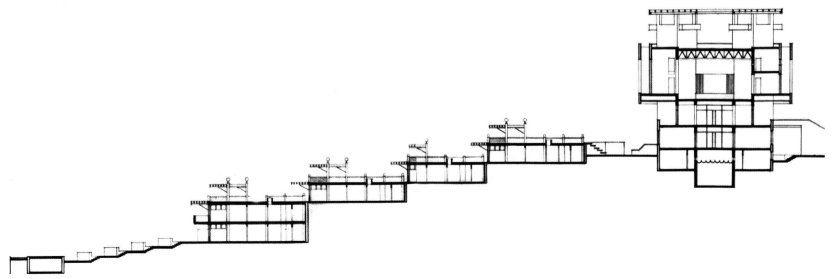

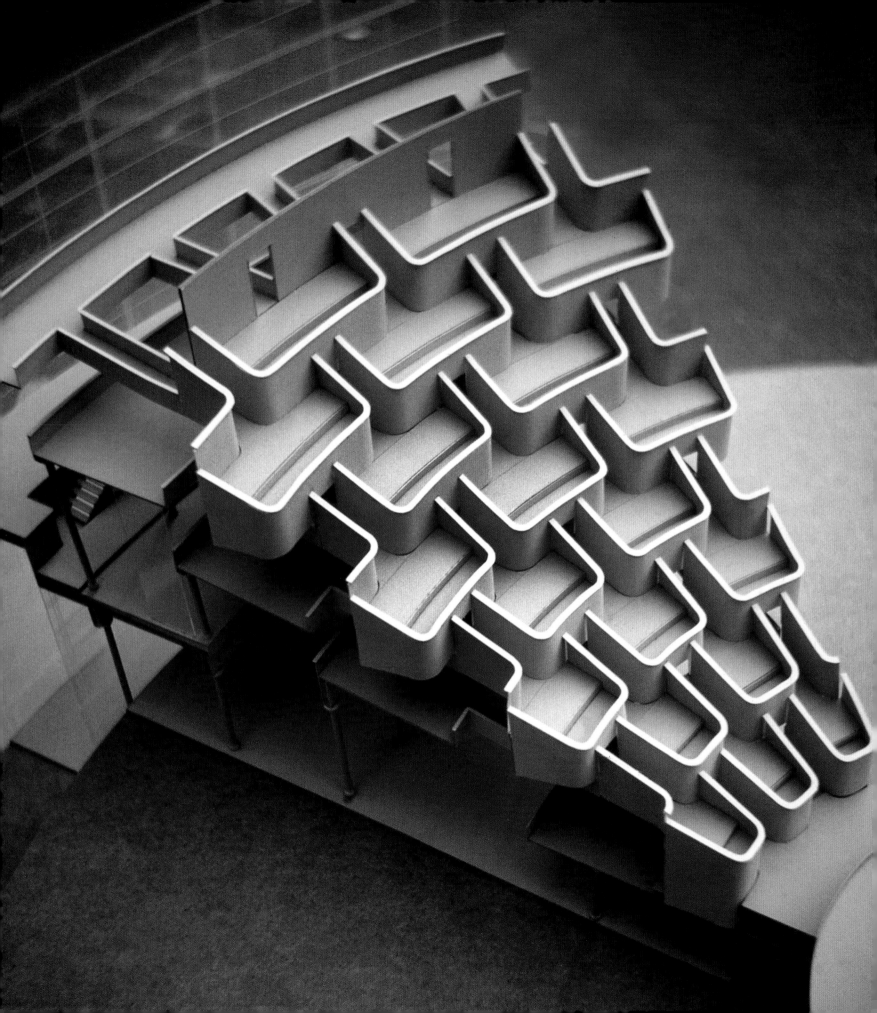

04

AMPHITHEATRE OF BOXES

The Amphitheatre of Boxes represents the synthesis of two classical types of auditorium: the ancient amphitheatre and the Italian tiered theatre. It preserves the sense of democracy of the former, with no seating hierarchy, while also providing each section of the audience with a feeling not only of privacy but also of belonging to the whole.

The auditorium part of the complex comprises differently sized seating sections, or boxes, for six to twenty people. The further away from the stage, the bigger the box. The tiers of boxes are laid out in a chessboard-like pattern, and each is built 1.2–1.25 m above the previous one. As a result, box entrances are 2.5 m high. Inside every box the back row is 30–35 cm higher than the front. This ensures a good view for all.

The boxes are accessed from a series of open walkways at the rear of the auditorium; these, in turn, lead to a central lobby. The movement of people along the walkways, visible to a height of several storeys, makes the intervals more theatrical, playing on the movement of theatregoers from the auditorium to the lobby and back. Moreover, the individual box entrances make it possible to use the boxes as additional stage areas in the midst of the audience.

The concept of the Amphitheatre of Boxes was the brainchild of Igor Yawein. Working on their father's creation in detail, Nikita and Oleg Yawein expect that, sooner or later, it will occupy its rightful place in the practice of building theatrical venues.

CLIENT: N/A
DESIGN: 1983
REALIZATION: N/A
TOTAL AREA: N/A

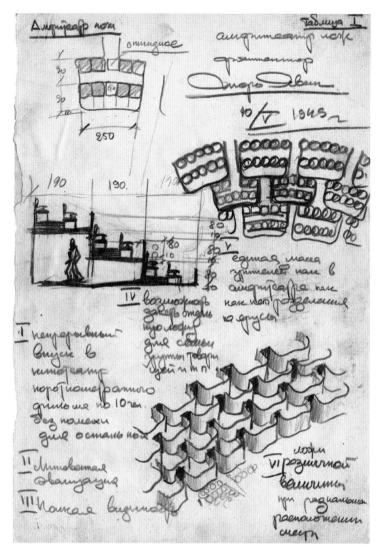

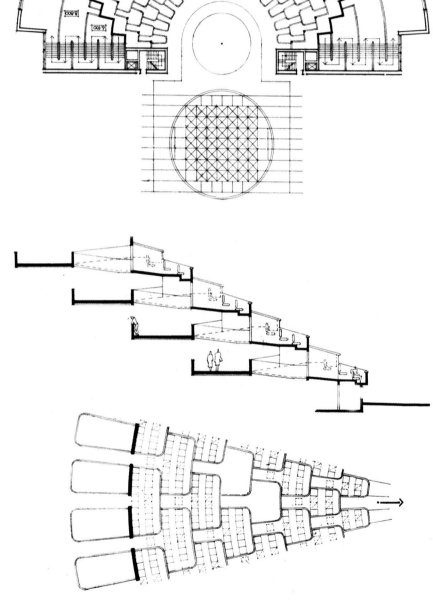

ABOVE
Igor Yawein's sketches for the
Amphitheatre of Boxes, 1945.

BELOW
Illustration showing the genesis of
the project: a combination of a tiered
theatre and an amphitheatre.

ABOVE, RIGHT
Plan of the auditorium and stage.

RIGHT
Cross-section and plan of the tiered
seating.

ABOVE
Mock-up of a section of the
auditorium.

RIGHT
A view of the same mock-up showing
the walkways at the back of the
auditorium.

Overhead view of the mock-up of
the auditorium and stage.

EXPLORATION OF
THE RUSSIAN NORTH

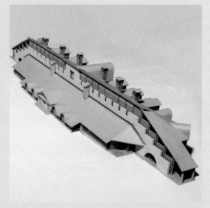

Through their father, Igor Yawein, a talented architect himself, Nikita and Oleg Yawein were exposed to architecture from an early age. The broad interest of their father helped them to develop an appreciation for a wide variety of architecture, from rural barns to urban palaces, much of which exists outside the conventional canon of modern architecture. Interested as much in mediaeval as in modern buildings, in folklore as much as in functionalism, the Yaweins have developed a generous and uncommonly inclusive perspective on architecture. This is reflected in the work of Studio 44.

By not distinguishing between old and new, or between architecture with and without an architect behind it, Studio 44 has been able to make a mark with work that is rooted in tradition yet also fully contemporary. This wide-ranging approach equipped the Yaweins with the right intellectual and architectural background to design the Kremlin Housing Community on the Solovetsky Islands in the Russian North (another project initiated before Studio 44 officially existed). On these islands, which became a UNESCO World Heritage Site in 1992, they had to find a balance between tradition and innovation, between respecting unique historical environments and contemporary needs. Just as in their early work, a clear geometry underlies each design, combined with a clever strategy of scaling parts of the buildings up and down, in order to integrate and contextualize them in such sensitive surroundings. The same scaling strategy was used for the country house the Yaweins made for themselves a few years later.

Hans Ibelings

05

KREMLIN HOUSING COMMUNITY

Located in the White Sea, the Solovetsky Islands are the pearl of the Russian North and a UNESCO World Heritage Site. A plot of land in the very heart of the islands was assigned to the Kremlin Housing Community, in the zone between Onega Bay and Holy Lake, not far from the fortified walls of Solovetsky Monastery (built sixteenth to nineteenth centuries).

The 'front line' of the settlement consists of buildings one and a half storeys high split into two apartments. The intervals between form a series of three-sided courtyards leading into the settlement, with larger, two-storey buildings for four families at their far side. This type of composition, with a graduated increase in the size of the buildings, is characteristic of housing communities in the Russian North, where granaries, bath houses and the like were usually built at the front. Behind them, in the second row, would be taller houses, and finally, in the centre, the church and bell tower.

All the buildings in the community are similar in form but have different floor plans and façades: the front-row buildings, facing the monastery, have finer articulation and detailing than the buildings in the second, third and fourth rows.

Solovetsky, Bolshoi Solovetsky Island, Arkhangelsk Region, Russia

CLIENT: Capital Construction Management, Arkhangelsk Region Executive Committee
DESIGN: 1988–9
REALIZATION: 1989–90 (phase 1)
TOTAL AREA: 4,078 sq m (46 apartments)

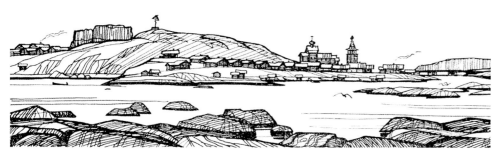

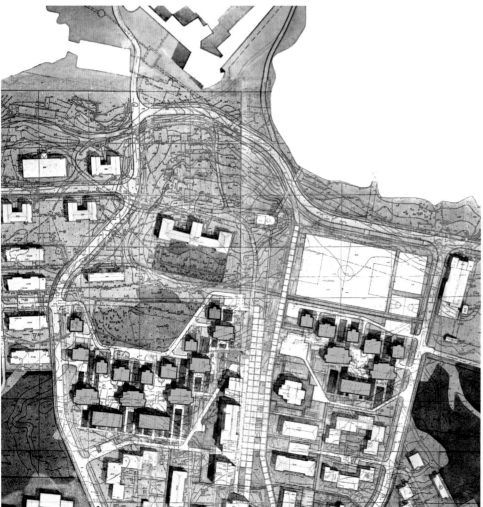

ABOVE
View of the housing community from
Holy Lake.

LEFT
Kovda rural locality. Illustration from
Yuri Ushakov, *Folk Architecture in the
Russian North*, 1982.

LEFT, BOTTOM
General plan.

BELOW
The design of the housing community
reflects the principle of 'kinship along
with diversity', a key feature of Russian
architecture.

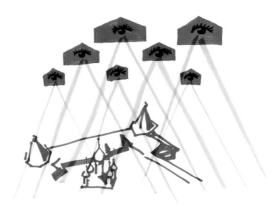

The front and second rows of the
housing community, facing Holy Lake.

Model of the housing community.

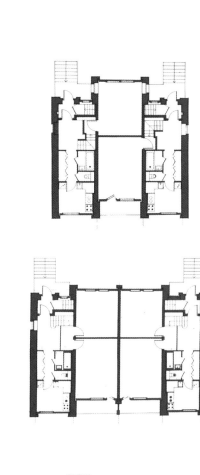

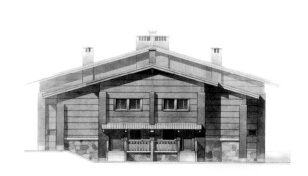

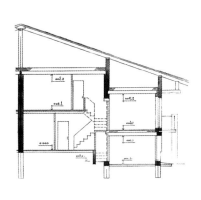
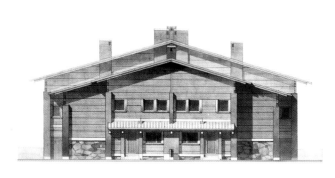

OPPOSITE
Plans, cross-sections and elevations of
the different types of accommodation
in the housing community.

RIGHT
The housing community in winter.

BELOW
Sketch of the apartment buildings
for four families.

06

NURSERY SCHOOL BUILDING, KREMLIN HOUSING COMMUNITY

The nursery school building is built around a square courtyard, which also serves as a playground. The courtyard has a roof lantern that rises above the rest of the building, thus marking the compositional heart of the complex.

This central feature is surrounded by four blocks: three nursery blocks – one for each of the three different age groups who attend the nursery – and one service block. Each nursery block, like a Russian doll, consists of three similarly shaped but differently sized structures. The largest ones contain playrooms and bedrooms, the medium-sized ones are verandas, and the smallest act as entrance porches. The porches extend outwards, giving the plan of the building a resemblance to a significant Old Russian symbol, the Solar Cross.

The service block (containing a kitchen, canteen, gym, medical centre and administrative offices) is in a standard rectangular structure. This single deviation from axial symmetry restrains the centrifugal dynamics of the floor plan created by the nursery blocks' 'rotation' around the courtyard.

Solovetsky, Bolshoi Solovetsky Island, Arkhangelsk Region, Russia

CLIENT: Capital Construction Management,
Arkhangelsk Region Executive Committee
DESIGN: 1989–91
REALIZATION: N/A
TOTAL AREA: N/A

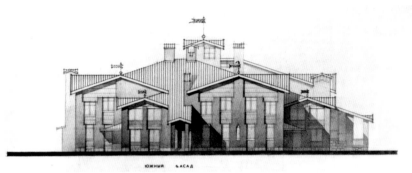

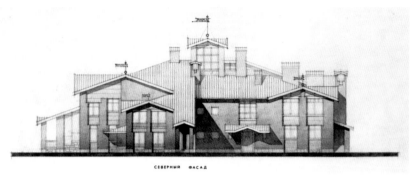

ABOVE, LEFT
South-facing façade.

ABOVE, RIGHT
North-facing façade.

BELOW, LEFT
First-floor plan.

BELOW, RIGHT
Second-floor plan.

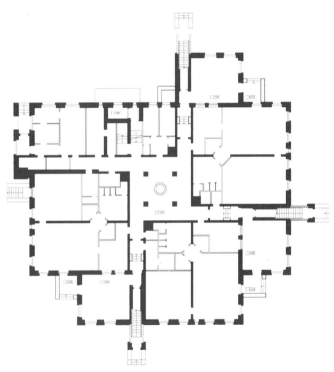

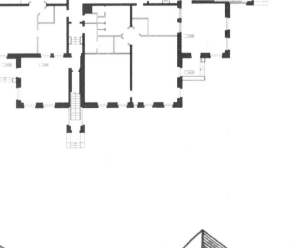

LEFT
The Russian doll-like formation of the nursery blocks, and their configuration within the plan of the building.

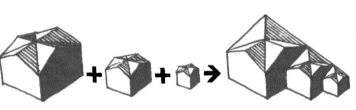

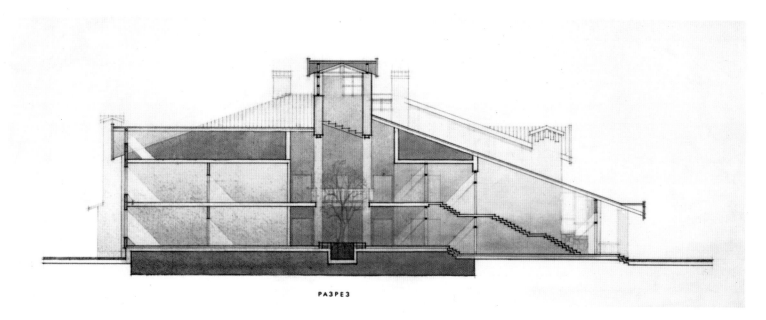

РАЗРЕЗ

ABOVE
Cross-section showing the inner
courtyard.

BELOW
A model of the nursery school.

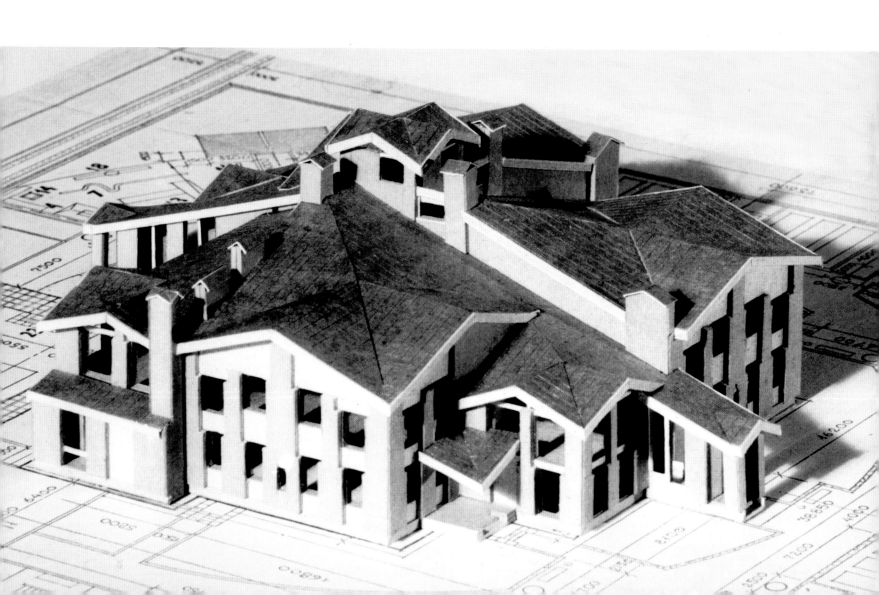

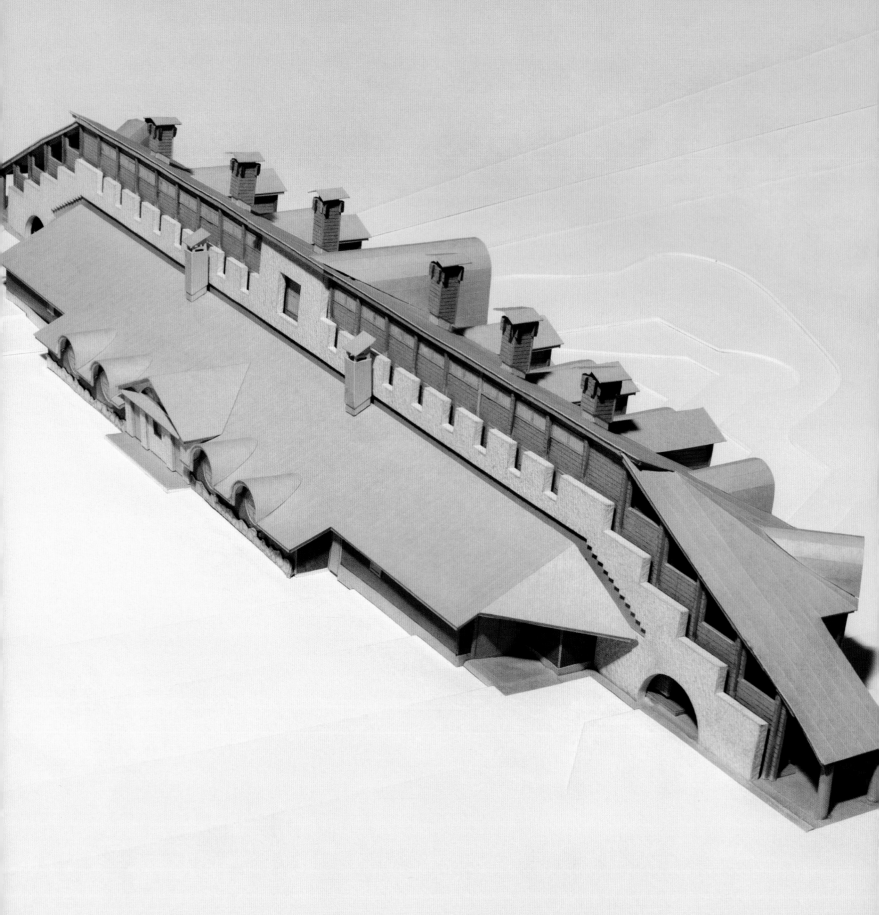

07

SOLOVKI AIRPORT HOTEL

Solovki Airport Hotel is large enough to accommodate the passengers from one or two eighteen-seater planes. The building comprises two long blocks stretching alongside the airfield. The single-storey stone block on the airport side houses the catering and services infrastructure. The two-storey wooden block contains thirty-four rooms, with all windows facing Solovetsky Monastery.

The blocks are connected by a covered passageway with upper side lighting. It is the hotel's main communications artery and has stairways at each end leading from street level to the first floor of the building, in line with traditional Russian architecture.

The building closely follows the line of the valley and looks as if it were composed of small wooden houses rising up on the slopes of the shallow ravine. Their inclined roofs are cut into the slanted surface of the larger roof, becoming porches over the outer stairways.

The way in which the walls of the building run alongside the airfield is designed to generate surprise. Passengers disembark from their aircraft, collect their luggage, cross the airfield, enter the hotel, check in … and all without even a hint of what it is they are here to see. Then they go to their room, approach the window, and there before their eyes is the incredible view of Solovetsky Monastery.

Solovetsky, Bolshoi Solovetsky Island, Arkhangelsk Region, Russia

CLIENT: Capital Construction Management,
Arkhangelsk Region Executive Committee
DESIGN: 1994–5
REALIZATION: N/A
TOTAL AREA: N/A

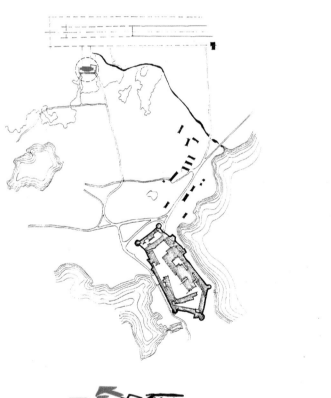

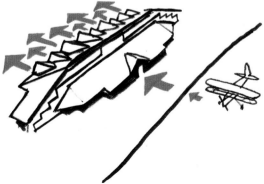

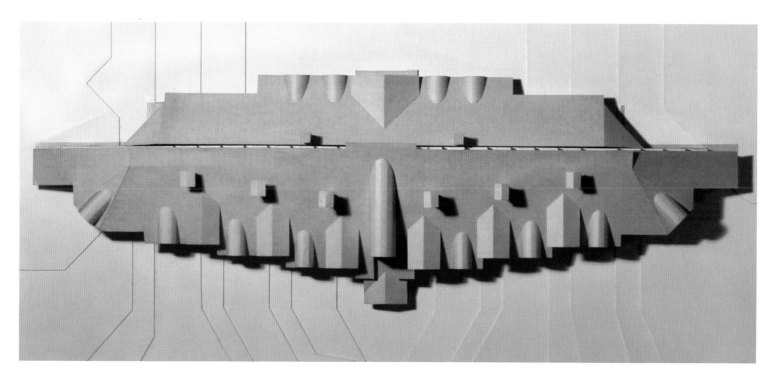

ABOVE
Model of the hotel, as seen from above.

BELOW
Lateral cross-section.

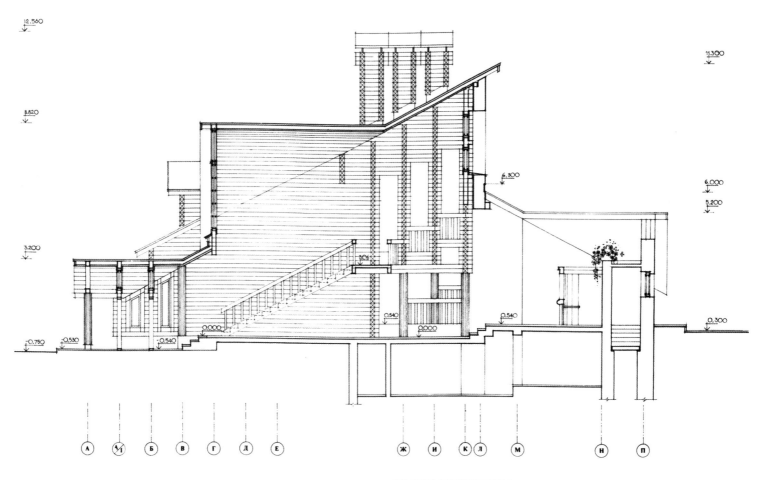

ABOVE
Longditudinal cross-section.

LEFT
First-floor plan.

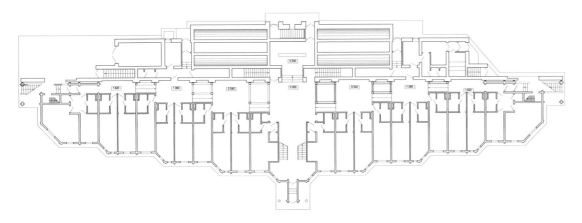

LEFT
Second-floor plan.

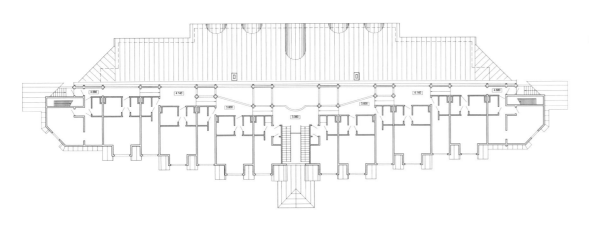

STUDIO 44

Model of the hotel, seen from the
accommodation side.

08

YAWEINS' COUNTRY HOUSE

Built of thick, 14 ×14-cm wooden beams, the house looks as though it is composed of three separate cottages: Nikita Yawein's own 4 × 4-m room, and the rooms of his mother and brother (3 × 3 m each). Each of these parts has its own façade, outside entrance and veranda. The fourth element of the building is the kitchen, which has an open terrace instead of a veranda.

The composition of the house is similar to that of the nursery school on the Solovetsky Islands (see page 57). However, owing to the house's function, there is a significant difference: here, the four main parts of the building are fused together in the centre and form a single space. This space is very large, making it possible to accommodate children, guests, houseplants, etc. on different levels.

The building's internal space is arranged in a spiral (from the multi-height dining/living room to the family members' private rooms) around a central supporting pillar. This is crowned by a crossbar with a tiny (1 × 1-m) viewing platform. From here, as if looking out from a crow's nest on a ship's mainmast, an impressive view opens out onto the Baltic Sea.

Pribylovo, Vyborg District, Leningrad Region, Russia

CLIENT: Yawein family
DESIGN: 1992–5
REALIZATION: 1996
TOTAL AREA: 165 sq m

ABOVE
The dining/living area is lit by multiple windows.

BELOW
Diagram showing the design scheme.

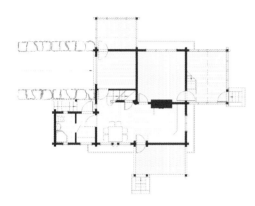

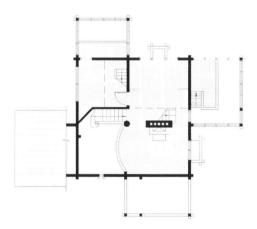

ABOVE
From top: cross-section, first-floor plan, second-floor plan.

RIGHT
Larch was the main building material used in the construction of the house.

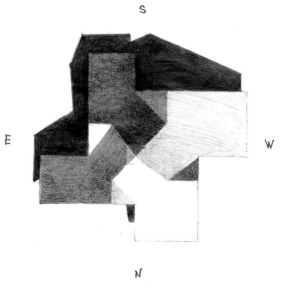

OPPOSITE, TOP
The north-facing façade of the
house, which looks towards
the Vyborg peninsula.

OPPOSITE, BOTTOM LEFT
View of the house from the south-east.

OPPOSITE, BOTTOM RIGHT
Diagram showing the house's
orientation.

RIGHT
View of the house from the south-west.

RIGHT, BOTTOM
View of the house from the north-east.

ST PETERSBURG AT THE
TURN OF THE 21ST CENTURY

The founding of Studio 44 coincided with, and was made possible by, the transition from the Soviet Union to the Russian Federation in 1991, during which Leningrad would become St Petersburg again. The new political, social and economic realities, despite all their flaws and problems, offered tremendous opportunities for Studio 44, especially in the mid-1990s. Much of the firm's work in its first years of existence was in and around St Petersburg, and included banks and office buildings, shopping centres, and new residential projects. During this time, architects, clients, investors and builders all had to invent, or reinvent, their methods of working. Realizing a building is a feat in any part of the world, but in St Petersburg around 2000, it must have been especially challenging, particularly if it stood out, such as the impressive Ladozhsky railway station or the main branch of the Sberbank, with its clever and playful mannerisms. Despite being completely different in its appearance, the Linkor Business Centre reveals a similar playfulness in another architectural vocabulary, underlining Studio 44's ability to speak more than one language.

Each of Studio 44's buildings in St Petersburg makes its mark on the urban landscape and contributes to the life of the city, sometimes in a modestly subdued manner, sometimes in a deliberately outspoken way. Yet, they do not impose themselves on the city as recognizable Studio 44 projects. In fact, they differ so much from one another that it is almost impossible to trace them back to the same source.

Hans Ibelings

09

CENTRAL BRANCH OF SBERBANK OF RUSSIA, ST PETERSBURG

Reconstruction and restoration of an architectural monument built in the first three decades of the 18th century

The building that houses Sberbank's operations management is a typical example of a nineteenth-century St Petersburg residential building, with a rather narrow outer façade and a chain of interconnected courtyards stretching back from the street. Renovations were carried out that conformed with the bank's vast building programme while still preserving the original façade and the structure of the courtyards.

The first courtyard, to where all the entrances and exits to the bank were relocated, with access via a narrow pavement, is treated as an open-air entrance hall. Its lower level resembles St Petersburg's embankments, with their descents down to the River Neva. As you look up, through the line of mighty rusticated columns to the freestanding stone trilithons on the edge of the roof, the language of architecture becomes ever more abstract, gradually harking back to its archaic origins. Around the second courtyard is a newer building with an atrium where, under three tiers of glass lights, the banking floor is located.

The building owes its integrity to the application of an $80 \times 80 \times 80$-cm architectural module. This module is clearly ingrained in the breakdown of all the building's layouts and façades, in the geometry of the granite columns, the floor patterns and the metal grilles. It causes the ordered compositions, with their cubes and cylinders, to resemble a children's game of blocks.

5 Furshtatskaya Street, St Petersburg, Russia

CLIENT: Sberbank of the Russian Federation in St Petersburg
DESIGN: 1996
REALIZATION: 1997–2000
TOTAL AREA: 4,161 sq m

ABOVE
View of the Sberbank building, overlooking Furshtatskaya Street.

FAR LEFT
St Anne's Lutheran Church. Etching by Aleksey Gornostayeva, 1834.

LEFT
Location of the Sberbank building.

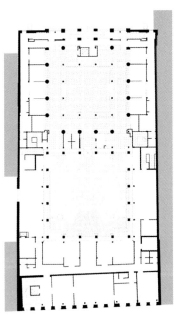

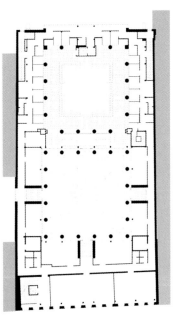

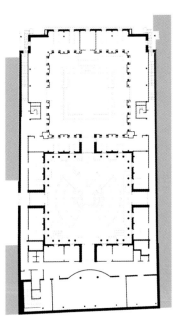

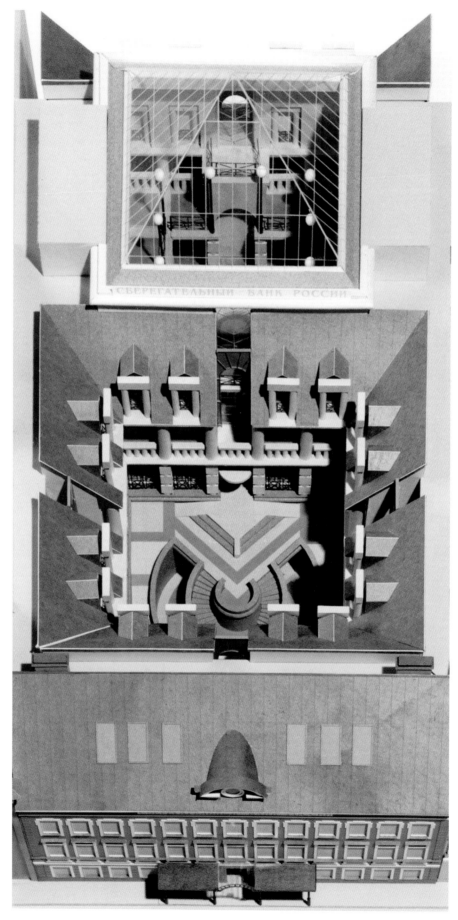

ABOVE
The open coutryard/grand vestibule
(main photo) and examples of the
St Petersburg architectural style that
inspired it.

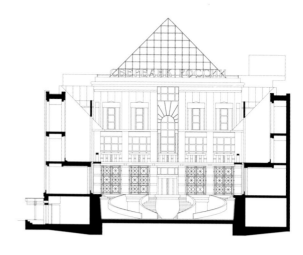

View of the internal courtyard.

Cross-section of the internal courtyard.

Façade treatments in the internal courtyard.

View from the roof of the building into the internal courtyard and beyond to St Anne's Church.

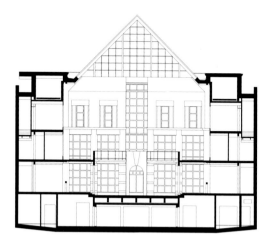

ABOVE, LEFT
St Petersburg motifs on the ground floor of the covered atrium.

ABOVE
Atrium cross-section.

LEFT
Examples of the rusticated columns.

OPPOSITE
View of the atrium's interior.

10
LADOZHSKY RAILWAY STATION

Ladozhsky is St Petersburg's sixth railway station, and the only one designed for through-trains. Its construction faced a rather complicated urban-development challenge. The designers found a way to realize the project's objectives, however, by proposing a construction that combines a station-tunnel and a station-bridge between two parts of the city.

The passenger area for long-distance trains is built over the tracks as a concourse, while the one for suburban trains is underground, giving the ground level over to the trains and public transport. The three station levels are connected both practically – with stairs, access ramps and escalators – and visually – with huge light shafts. Physical representations of the movement of passengers, transport and luggage –

projecting beams and small bridges, the transparent shells of lifts and crossings – occur throughout the station and form a layer of twenty-first-century imagery. At the same time, the architectural imagery of the building encompasses many historical prototypes, from the train sheds of the late nineteenth century to the Roman baths and triumphal arches that inspired the architects of the earliest railway stations.

The façade of the building, with its three stained-glass windows under triangular roofs, framed by two fortress-like towers, is comparable to the inhabited bridges of European cities. In this way, the architecture of the station embodies its function: a bridge between two large city districts separated by railway tracks.

73 Zanevsky Prospekt, St Petersburg, Russia

CLIENT: Ministry of Transport of the Russian Federation
DESIGN: 2001–2
REALIZATION: 2001–3
TOTAL AREA: 33,076 sq m

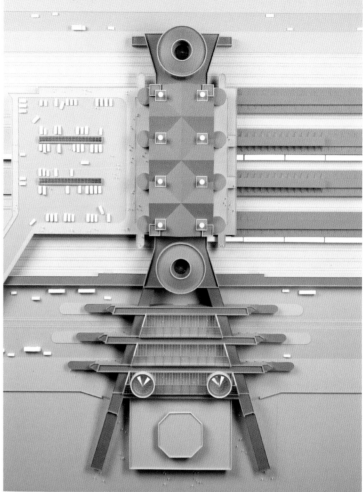

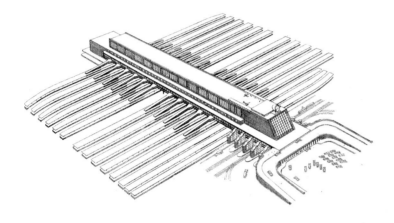

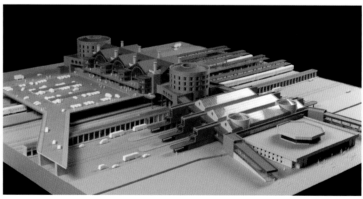

ABOVE

From top: tender proposal for Nikolaievsky (Moscow) station by Ivan Fomin, 1912, a prototype for Ladozhsky station; Pennsylvania Station, New York, 1911; design of Central (Kursky Region) station in Moscow by Igor Yawein, 1932; degree project on Ladozhsky station by Nikita Yawein, 1976.

ABOVE

Two views of the model of the station.

OPPOSITE

Passenger hall for intercity trains.

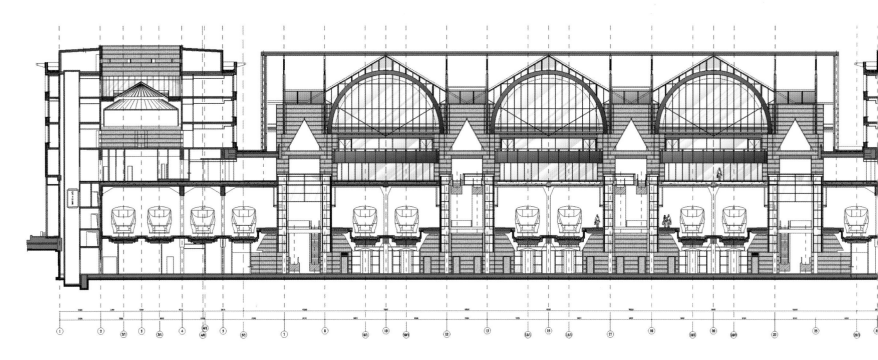

ABOVE
Longitudinal cross-section.

LEFT
The station also acts as a bridge
and tunnel.

BELOW
Platform-level plan.

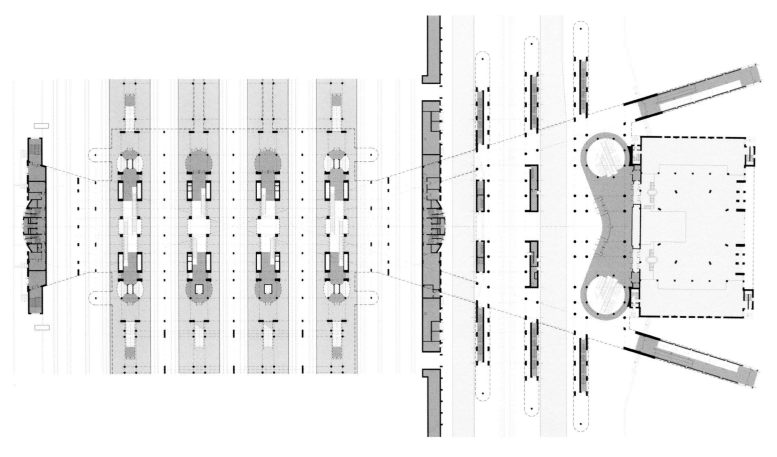

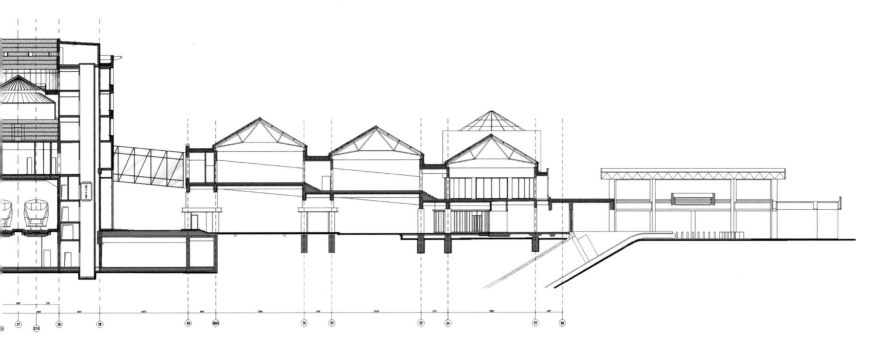

BELOW
Plan of the passenger area for intercity
trains (concourse level).

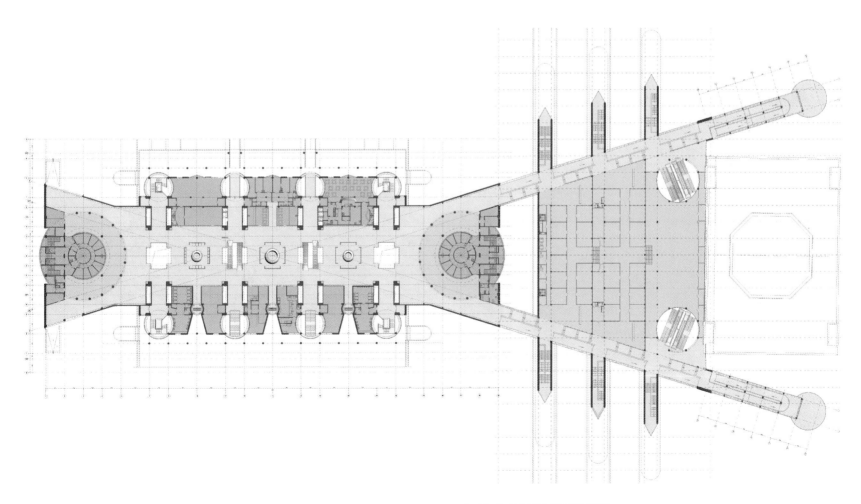

LADOZHSKY RAILWAY STATION

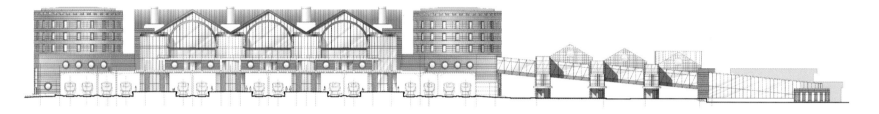

STUDIO 44

ABOVE, TOP
View of the station from the
entry ramp.

ABOVE
North elevation.

LEFT
Façade detail.

OPPOSITE
View of the station from the city-
transport approach zone.

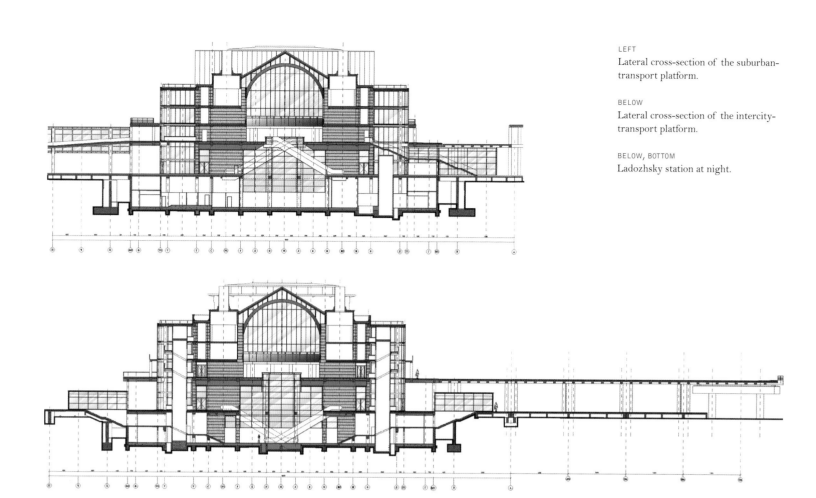

LEFT
Lateral cross-section of the suburban-transport platform.

BELOW
Lateral cross-section of the intercity-transport platform.

BELOW, BOTTOM
Ladozhsky station at night.

The main passenger hall features twenty-six metal arches weighing approximately 174 tonnes.

Details of the metal arches.

View of the main station entrace at night.

11

RESIDENTIAL BUILDING, KRESTYANSKY LANE

The architecture of this building comprises, in condensed, concentrated form, a range of motifs, approaches and spatial arrangements that were characteristic of St Petersburg's Petrograd Side in the late nineteenth and early twentieth century. In plan, the building resembles a butterfly, with an arch linking the 'wings'. This arch is the compositional centre of the façade, the fabric of which is a dense collection of faceted bay windows and towers, giving it the appearance of a Gothic portal. But this portal has been built to a fantastic scale – the scale of a cour d'honneur. The whole building is an amalgamation of textures: the brick and plaster surfaces are laced with areas of glass and metal. In this way, the various elements of the building provide a link to its historic context while the concept as a whole remains completely unique.

3 Krestyansky Lane, St Petersburg, Russia

CLIENT: Baltic Construction Company – Industrial Civil Construction
DESIGN: 2001–2
REALIZATION: 2002–4
TOTAL AREA: 7,645 sq m

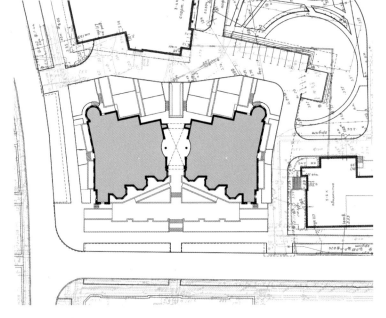

Examples of buildings in Petrograd Side from the beginning of the twentieth century.

Site plan.

Diagram showing the design scheme.

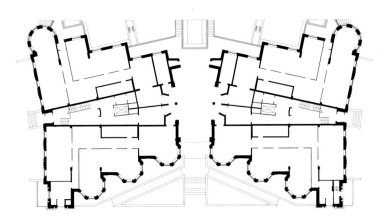
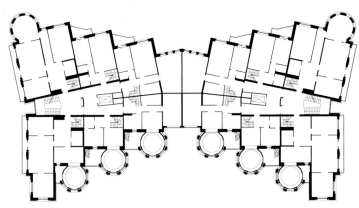

First-floor plan.

Sixth-floor plan.

Two different views of the building, including (top) a view of the main façade.

12

NEVSKY 38 BUSINESS CENTRE

Reconstruction and restoration of an architectural monument built in the first three decades of the eighteenth century

The building at Nevsky 38 was erected three hundred years ago. It has been rebuilt more than ten times in its history and suffered severe fire damage in 1994. During its reconstruction by Studio 44, everything of no value was removed, the load-bearing walls were reinforced, and everything of significance was restored: the vaulted eighteenth-century cellars (by Mikhail Zemtsov); the classical, early nineteenth-century façades (Carlo Rossi); the iron colonnades of 1881 (Heinrich Prang); and the double-height banking floor of the former Volga-Kama Bank, built in the spirit of late French classicism (1898, Leonti Benois).

The inner courtyard, the only place where new construction was possible, was transformed into a covered atrium, snugly surrounded by office blocks. The inspiration for turning the complexities and limitations of this tall, narrow courtyard – practically no more than a gap – into something of artistic value was the multi-tiered Roman aqueduct. A network of steel bridges and walkways traversing the courtyard's void was added to the building's stone arcades. In this way, the building's many cultural layers, located at various points throughout the structure, were united, both functionally and visibly.

The notional centre of the composition is the restored historic strongroom, complete with a series of sturdy bolts on its steel door. The only access to the strongroom is via a narrow bridge, which always attracts the attention of passersby.

38 Nevsky Prospekt, St Petersburg, Russia

CLIENT: PSB
DESIGN: 2000–3
REALIZATION: 2001–4
TOTAL AREA: 14,500 sq m

c. 1740, Mikhail Zemtsov

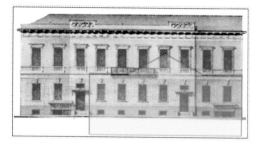

c. 1800, architect unknown

1834, Carlo Rossi

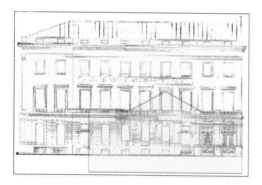

1881, Heinrich Prang

1890, Leonti Benois

History of the building's architecture.

No. 38 Nevsky Prospekt in the first half of the twentieth century.

The aftermath of the fire that destroyed the building in 1994.

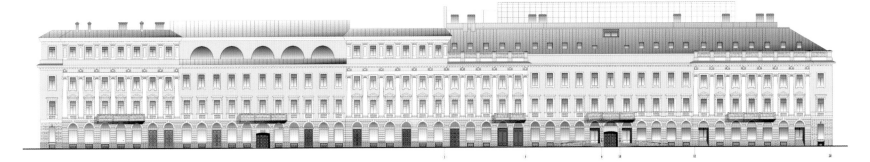

ABOVE
Mikhailovsky Street elevation.

BELOW
View of the building from Nevsky Prospekt.

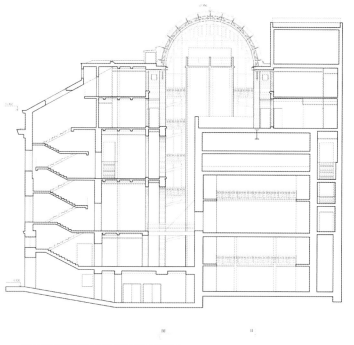

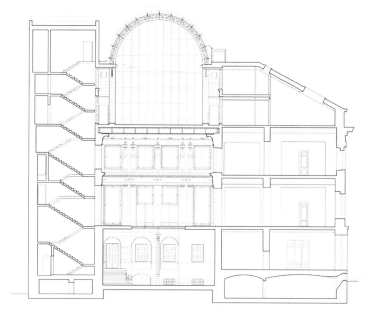

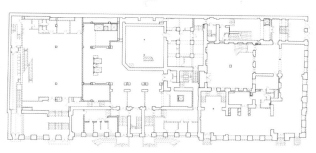

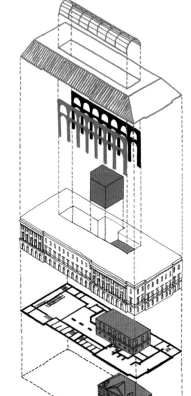

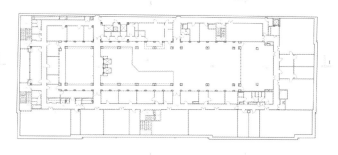

ABOVE, LEFT
Latitudinal cross-section of the building.

ABOVE
Longitudinal cross-section of the Benois Hall.

FAR LEFT
First-floor plan, second-floor plan and plan of the attic floor.

LEFT
Restoration and construction scheme.

ABOVE
Historic interiors after the restoration.

RIGHT
The Benois Hall after restoration.

LEFT
Views of the restored strongroom
and arcades.

OPPOSITE, TOP
Longitudinal cross-section of
the atrium.

OPPOSITE, BOTTOM
Atrium circulation system:
side galleries, lift and bridges.

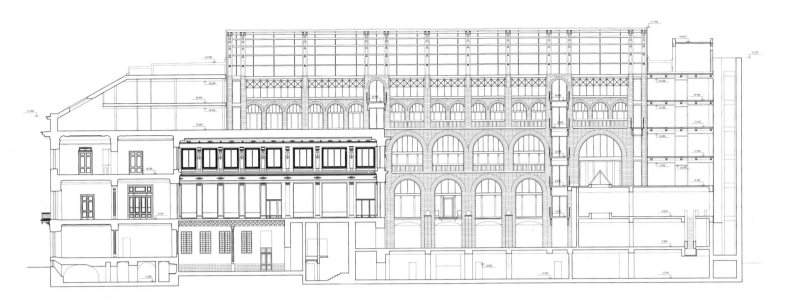

LEFT
A single bridge leads to the strongroom.

ABOVE
Details of the strongroom's locking mechanism.

OPPOSITE
Café on one of the upper levels of the atrium.

LEFT, TOP AND BOTTOM
Two of the bridges that cross
the atrium.

OPPOSITE
View of the atrium.

13

RESIDENTIAL BUILDING, 10TH SOVIETSKAYA STREET

This seventy-unit apartment building is located in an area between the prestigious central neighbourhoods of St Petersburg and the industrial zone. In the 1920s and 1930s the masters of Russian constructivism worked here, in search of new aesthetics at the intersection of such seemingly different styles as classicism and the avant-garde.

The building is an attempt not only to interpret the work of the constructivists but also to continue along their path. It has the recognizable features of constructivism: flat triangles and the arches of bay windows, glazed balconies and smooth, sterile walls, thin column bases, and, finally, a sharp, acute-angled corner, confidently cutting through space. In the style of the constructivists, the building is composed of basic geometric forms: rectangular and triangular prisms and cylinders.

It is not, however, a montage of constructivism. The assembly principle is different: although the constituent elements seem independent of one another, they all follow the main theme, coming together to form a single whole. The walls of the building 'bend' and 'break', but not to demonstrate a shifting world order. They are simply, like any living organism might, reacting to the pressure exerted by the large, circular courtyard inside.

4/6, 10th Sovietskaya Street, St Petersburg, Russia

CLIENT: GRST-1
DESIGN: 2003–5
REALIZATION: 2005–6
GROSS FLOOR AREA: 10,762 sq m

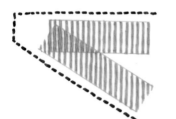

ABOVE
Moisayenko Street elevation.

LEFT
Sequence showing the creation of the building's form.

LEFT, BOTTOM
Site plan.

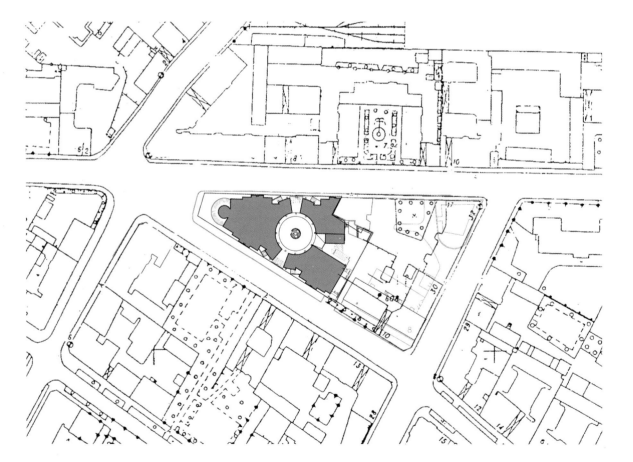

ABOVE
View of the building from the nearby
road junction.

RIGHT
Plan of the building at 16.8 m.

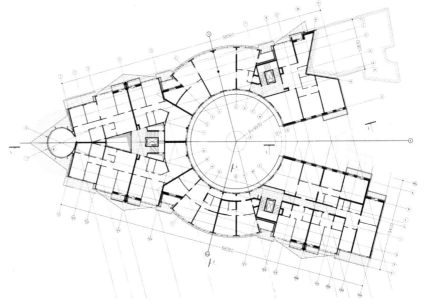

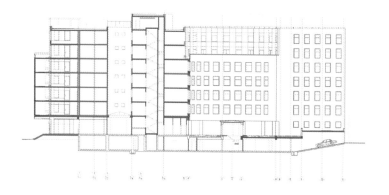

ABOVE
View of the building from
10th Sovietskaya Street.

BELOW
First-floor plan and standard floor plan.

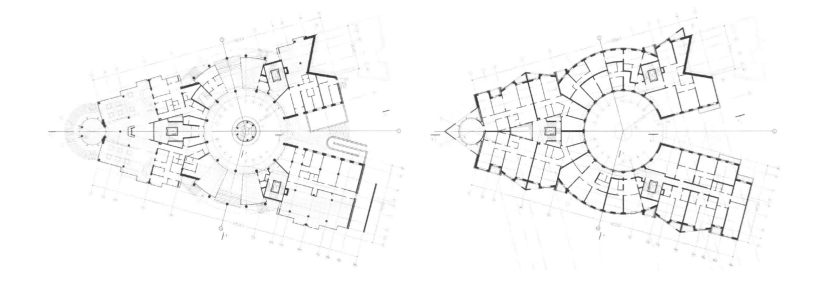

14

STUDIO 44 OFFICES

Reconstructed building from early 20th century

Studio 44's new offices are located in the very heart of St Petersburg, a hundred metres from Preobrazhenskaya Square and the Empire-style Transfiguration Cathedral (1829, Vasily Stasov), in a building constructed in 1911. The original, three-storey building was not large enough to accommodate the entire practice, and so, during the conversion process, a mansard was added.

The smooth curve of the mansard conceals the double height of the addition (7 m). Nine strong, glued timber beams – each of which is made of five parts, three straight and two curved –

characterize the structure and lend a distinctly natural feel to the interior.

The mansard is asymmetrical: the north side of the roof is steep, with sloped ribbon windows, while the south side falls away more more gradually with fewer windows. This provides the workspace with the maximum amount of daylight while protecting it from the heat of the summer.

The office space on the lower floors is very different from the mansard. Its design is that of a classical enfilade, with walls painted in rich, bright colours.

3 Manezhny Lane, St Petersburg, Russia

CLIENT: Studio 44 Architects
DESIGN: 2006–8
REALIZATION: 2007–9
GROSS FLOOR AREA: 1,186 sq m

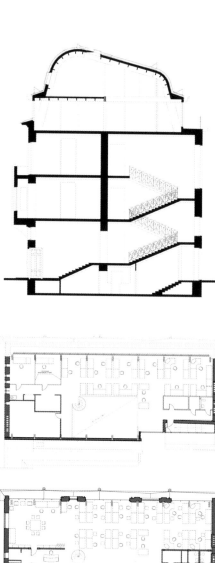

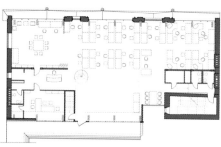

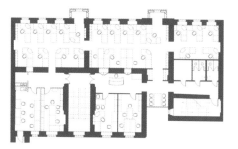

View of the offices from Manezhny
Lane with the Transfiguration
Cathedral in the background.

ABOVE
View from Manezhny Lane showing
the profile of the added mansard.

ABOVE
From top: cross-section showing the
stairs; plan of the upper-mansard level;
plan of the first mansard level; plan of
the third floor.

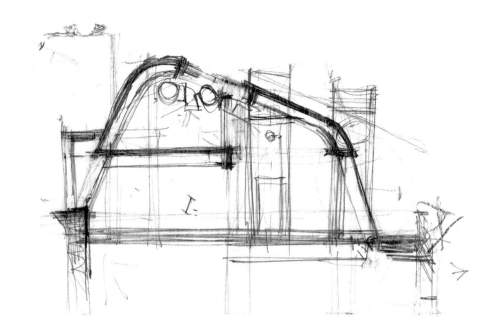

FAR LEFT, TOP AND BOTTOM
A round window looks out towards the Transfiguration Cathedral.

LEFT
Mansard interior.

LEFT, BOTTOM
Communal and meeting areas.

15

LINKOR
BUSINESS CENTRE

Reconstructed buildings from the 1970s

Built on the framework of two former industrial buildings, Linkor Business Centre resembles a ship adrift. It owes its look to the nearby cruiser *Aurora* and, perhaps even more so, to the client's desire to make its building resemble a vessel that can withstand any financial storm.

The form of a ship is one of the most popular images and motifs in contemporary architecture. In this case, however, it also comes with a range of functional advantages. First, the construction of the building as a ship on bolsters means there is room for a large visitors' car park underneath, thus preventing visitors from losing their way in the labyrinths of an underground car park. Secondly, the vessel's shape – wide at the bottom and smoothly tapering towards the top –

corresponds perfectly to the demand for different types of office space. The economical 'hold', containing offices with flexible floor plans, is ideally suited to large sub-divisions of major companies. Smaller and more expensive offices are located further up, with the most expensive higher still.

From the car park, visitors walk straight into the atrium that connects the two blocks. Here, because of the sloping walls and wave-like ceiling, it can feel as if you are underwater, in between two ships.

From the embankment, the building looks a little unfinished, since its glass shell does not run to the end of the 'decks', leaving the structure exposed. It is as though it is not yet ready to slide down the slipway into the water.

34 Petrogradskaya Embankment, St Petersburg, Russia

CLIENT: BFA Development
DESIGN: 2004–7
REALIZATION: 2007–9
GROSS FLOOR AREA: 23,183 sq m

LEFT
One of the original office buildings
in the 1970s.

BELOW
Design scheme.

BELOW
Cross-section of a wooden ship.

BELOW, BOTTOM
View of the Linkor Business Centre
from the Neva River. In the foreground
is the cruiser *Aurora*.

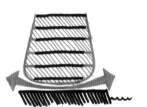

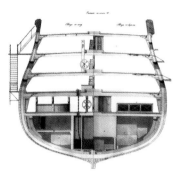

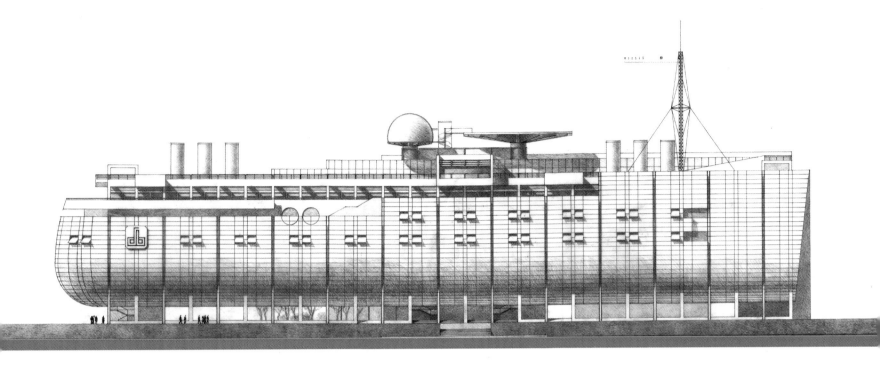

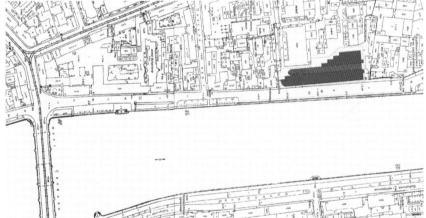

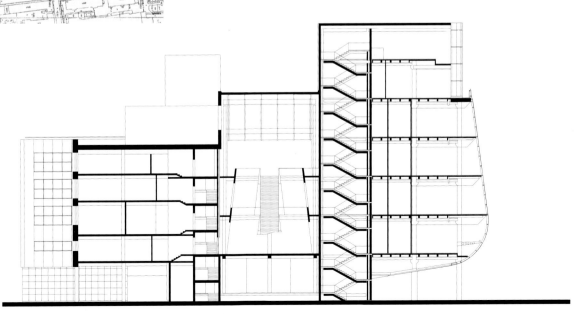

RIGHT
Latitudinal cross-section.

ABOVE, LEFT
The curved glass of the lower main façade – the 'bottom of the ship'.

ABOVE AND LEFT
Design sketches.

ABOVE
View of the business centre in winter.

RIGHT
Second-floor plan.

RIGHT, BOTTOM
First-floor plan.

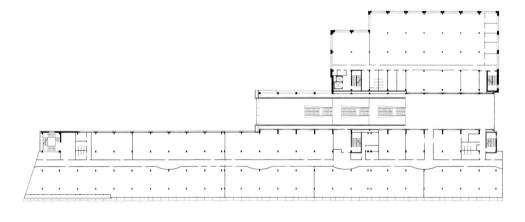

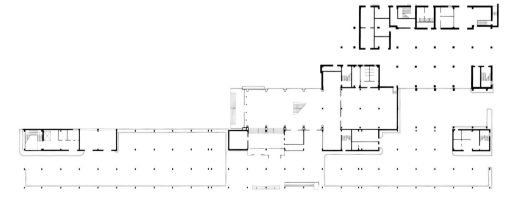

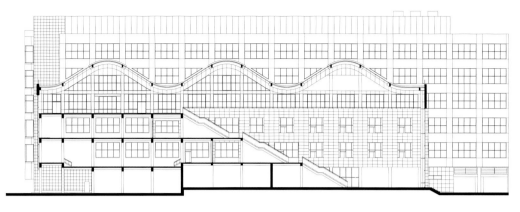

LEFT
Longitudinal cross-section of
the atrium.

LEFT, BOTTOM
Design sketch.

16

NEW PETERHOF HOTEL

A plot of land in the very heart of Peterhof, close to the famous eighteenth-century palaces and parks, was chosen as the site for this 150-room hotel. Local by-laws prohibit the construction of buildings more than 30 m in length and 12 m in height, so the building was designed in the form of six separate accommodation blocks, 24 × 24 × 11 m each. They are connected by a single-storey podium that houses all the hotel's facilities: reception desk, administration and services, restaurant, café, bar, fitness centre and a small conference hall.

The accessible roof area of the podium is designed in the form of an 'inner street', with glass lights illuminating the hotel lobby below. This 'street' is oriented towards the Cathedral of Sts Peter and Paul, built in 1905 in the Old Russian style. The 8-m gaps between the accommodation blocks are lined with sloping lawns. In this way, the hotel, which is actually quite spacious, gives the impression of being an intimate arrangement of small landscaped structures.

40/16 Sankt-Peterburgsky Prospekt, Petrodvortsovy District (Peterhof), St Petersburg, Russia

CLIENT: INTEKO
DESIGN: 2004–6
REALIZATION: 2006–10
TOTAL AREA: 14,921 sq m

ABOVE
Elevation along Sankt-Peterburgsky
Prospekt, with the Cathedral of Sts
Peter and Paul to the left of the hotel.

BELOW
View of the hotel from Holguin Pond.

ABOVE
View from Sankt-Peterburgsky
Prospekt.

LEFT
Site plan.

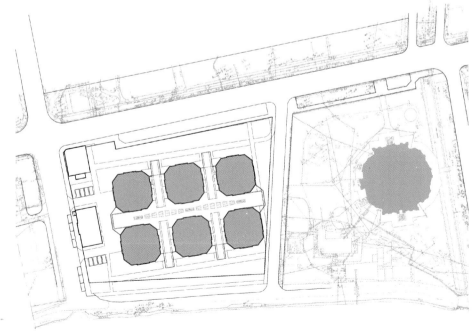

NEW PETERHOF HOTEL

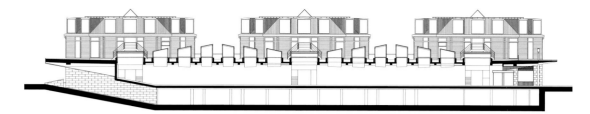

LEFT
Longitudinal cross-section.

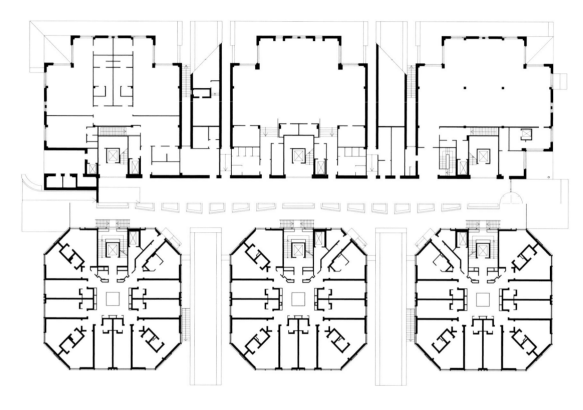

LEFT
Combined plan of the first and
second floors.

BELOW, LEFT AND RIGHT
Access ramp between two of
the accommodation blocks.

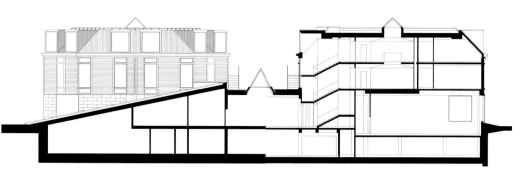

ABOVE
Latitudinal cross-section.

BELOW
External view of one of the
accommodation blocks.

RIGHT
View of the gallery inside one of
the accommodation blocks.

21ST-CENTURY PROJECTS
AND BUILDINGS

In recent years, the number, scale and complexity of Studio 44's projects have all increased. Its geographical range is now much larger too, with projects in Sochi, Moscow, Kaliningrad and Astana in Kazakhstan.

One of the best known of these recent projects is the transformation of the East Wing of the General Staff Building in St Petersburg into an extension of the Hermitage Museum. The careful mix of restoration, renovation and intervention has led to a rich and complex result, where old and new not only coexist but also are unified in a rare architectural synthesis. The Hermitage extension is the most conspicuous of a significant number of cultural and community projects designed by Studio 44, ranging from the Scientific and Technical Museum in Tomsk to the Zhastar Youth Palace and Palace of Schoolchildren, both in Astana. With the campus of the Graduate School of Management of the St Petersburg State University and the Boris Eifman Dance Academy, Studio 44 has also established a position in the world of designing for education.

Together, these projects show a shift from private commissions to an increasingly public domain, where the architecture affects a large number of people, becoming more 'of the people'. For decades, everything in Russia was unavoidably of the people, and in the first few years after the fall of communism, there was an understandable allergy to anything collective. But if Studio 44 were seen as a pars pro toto, its growing number of public commissions could be interpreted as proof that, after two decades of a near absence of public projects, the pendulum is beginning to swing the other way.

Hans Ibelings

17

THE STATE HERMITAGE MUSEUM IN THE EAST WING OF THE GENERAL STAFF BUILDING

An early 19th-century architectural monument restored and adapted to serve a new function

The General Staff Building (also known as the Ministry Building; 1830, Carlo Rossi) is one of the symbols of the Russian Empire, and one of the pinnacles of the Russian Empire style. Following the reconstruction of the East Wing, it now houses a collection of art dating from the nineteenth century to today.

Five of the inner courtyards of the building, which is a whole neighbourhood in itself, have been enclosed under glass roofs and transformed into the New Grand Enfilade. This consists of a sequence of large exhibition rooms, built into the transverse sections at first-floor level, as well as hanging gardens on platforms. The architecture of the exhibition rooms is designed to facilitate the transformation of the exhibition space: the various ways in which the double doors and walls can be configured enable flexible display changes, and either isolate each room or join them together again in an enfilade.

The ground floor of the complex is designed as a sort of enclosed continuation of Palace Square, a city forum with museum shops, an information centre, cloakroom, ticket office, lecture theatre, etc. The permanent exhibition is located on the first, second, third and fourth floors. The rooms in the New Grand Enfilade, together with the display of impressionist paintings, are provided with natural light through the clerestories in the ceiling.

6–8 Palace Square, St Petersburg, Russia

CLIENT: St Petersburg Foundation for Investment Projects
DESIGN: 2002–9
REALIZATION: 2008–14
TOTAL AREA: 60,473 sq m

ABOVE, TOP
Part of the main façade of the General
Staff Building.

ABOVE
Aerial photographs of Palace Square
(top and bottom), and of the East Wing
of the General Staff Building before
and after construction of the New
Grand Enfilade (left and right).

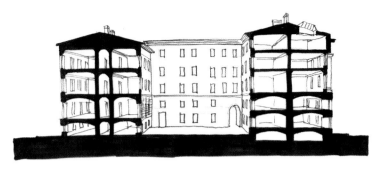

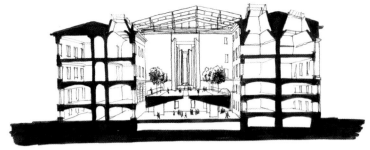

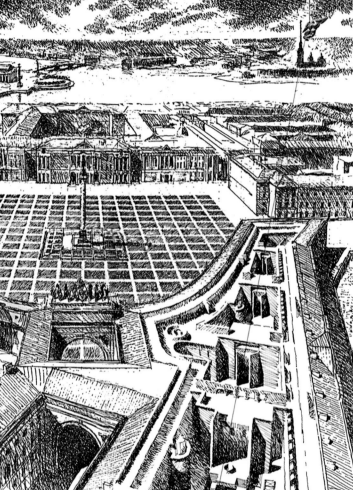

ABOVE, LEFT AND RIGHT
Latitudinal cross-sections of the East Wing before and after reconstruction.

LEFT
The New Grand Enfilade follows the tapered layout of the East Wing, the central axis of which was designed to line up with the spire of Sts Peter and Paul Cathedral.

BELOW
Diagram showing the orientation of the triumphal arches in relation to Palace Square, and the convergence of perspective through the East Wing.

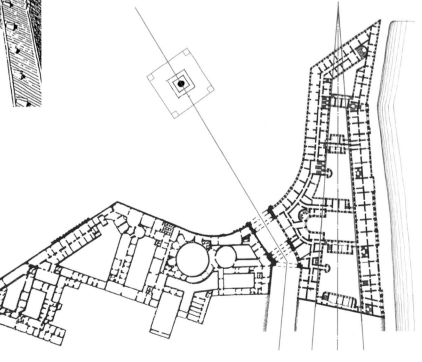

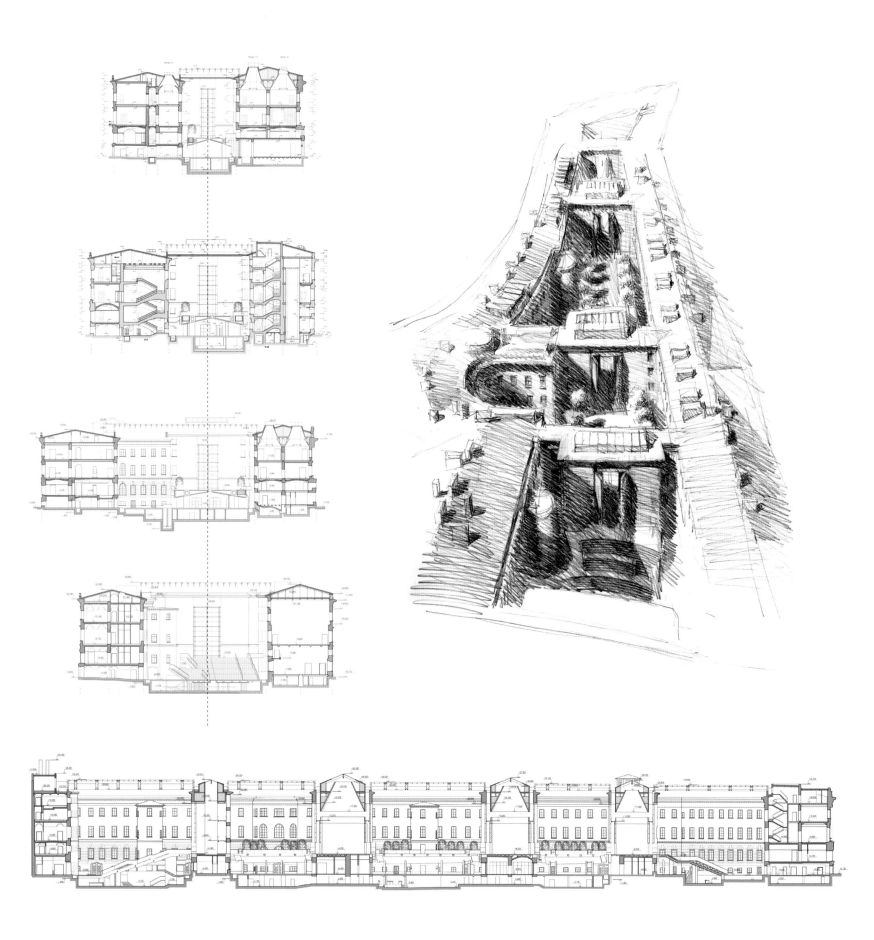

OPPOSITE, LEFT
Latitudinal cross-sections of the four
internal courtyards of the East Wing.

OPPOSITE, RIGHT
Sketch of the New Grand Enfilade.

OPPOSITE, BOTTOM
Longitudinal cross-section of the
New Grand Enfilade along its axis.

THIS PAGE
First-floor plan.

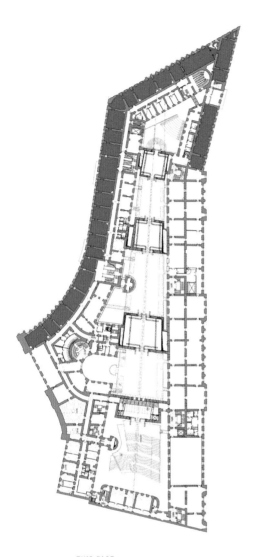

One of the grand enfilades of the
former Ministry of Foreign Affairs
after restoration (left) and their location
on a plan of the East Wing (above).

The dining room (top) and ballroom of
the former Ministry of Foreign Affairs.

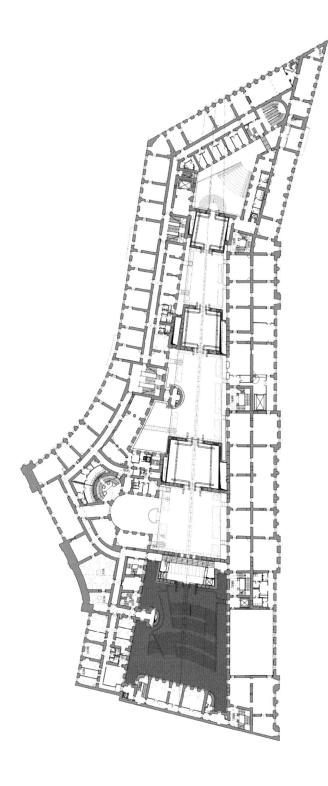

The entrance courtyard (right) and its location on a plan of the East Wing (above).

The amphitheatre-like 'triumphal' staircase in the entrance courtyard.

OPPOSITE, TOP LEFT AND TOP RIGHT
The triumphal staircase can be used as a recreational space and assembly hall.

OPPOSITE, BOTTOM LEFT
Model of the triumphal staircase.

OPPOSITE, BOTTOM RIGHT
Sketch of the triumphal staircase.

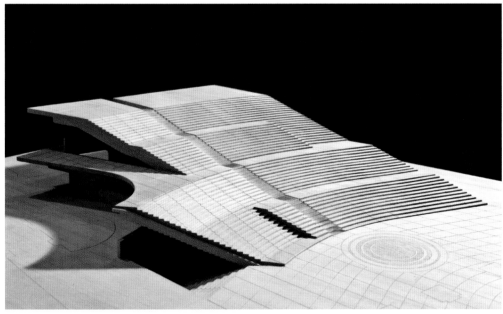

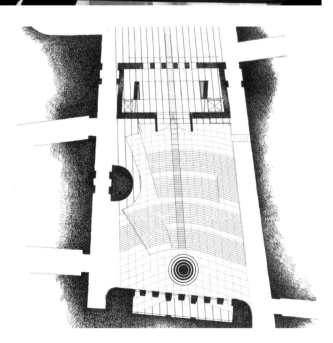

OPPOSITE
The entrance courtyard in the evening, lit by artificial light.

ABOVE
The cloakroom area below the triumphal staircase.

RIGHT
The triumphal staircase seen from behind.

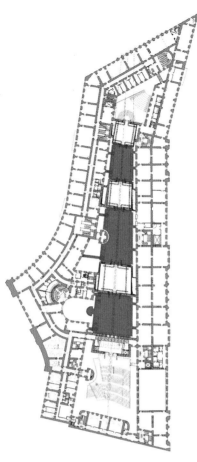

One of the three covered courtyards
used as exhibition spaces (left) and their
location on a plan of the East Wing
(above).

View through the exhibition halls and
covered courtyards of the New Grand
Enfilade.

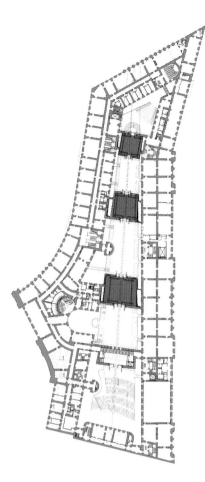

One of the exhibition halls of the New Grand Enfilade (left) and their location on a plan of the East Wing (above).

ABOVE, LEFT AND RIGHT
The doors and walls of the exhibition
halls can be configured in a number of
different ways.

RIGHT
Cross-section of an exhibition hall.

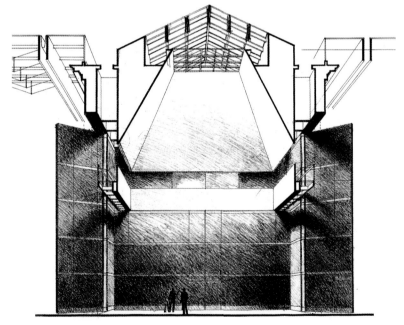

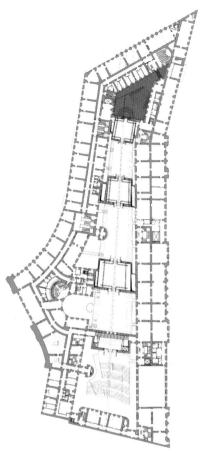

THIS PAGE
The 'Singers'' staircase in the triangular courtyard at the eastern-most end of the New Grand Enfilade (left) and its location on a plan of the East Wing (above).

OPPOSITE, TOP LEFT
The Singers' staircase seen from the cloakroom area below.

OPPOSITE, TOP RIGHT
View through the New Grand Enfilade from the Singers' staircase. The glazed area indicates the position of the building's central axis.

OPPOSITE, BOTTOM LEFT
The cloakroom area underneath the Singers' staircase.

OPPOSITE, BOTTOM RIGHT
The lower part of the Singers' staircase forms a small amphitheatre with two levels of seating.

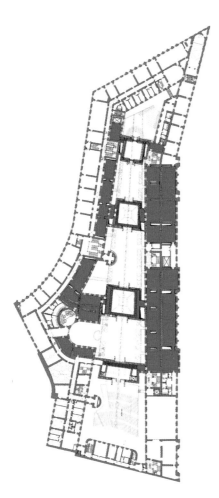

View of the Shchukin-Morozov Gallery (right), home to post-impressionist and impressionist masterpieces, and its location on a plan of the East Wing (above).

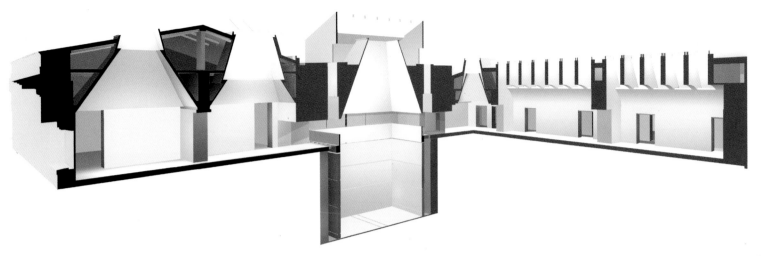

Photographs and diagrams of
the overhead lighting schemes.

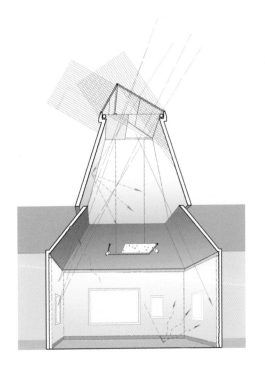

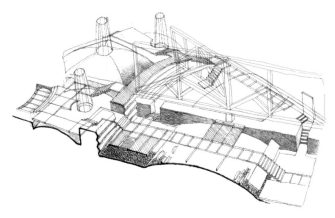

ABOVE, TOP
Cross-section of the triumphal arches.

ABOVE
Axonometric diagram of one of the exhibition spaces in the triumphal arches.

ABOVE AND OPPOSITE
Views of the exhibition spaces inside the triumphal arches.

18

ASTANA RAILWAY STATION

The station is designed to serve as the main land gateway to Astana. Its location at the intersection of major transport networks – railway, road and light railway – make it a major transport hub. For this reason, in addition to the station itself, there is a commercial building comprising a hotel, a business centre, and a shopping and entertainments complex. Located on either side of the railway tracks, the station and commercial building are connected by subways and overhead galleries.

The passenger areas of the station are situated on a concourse above the tracks. Pedestrians can ascend to the level of the central hall (+12 m) using the low steps in the terraced station square, or by travelator. Access to the underground public-transport stops (−3.3 m), the platforms (+4.2 m), the light railway (+8.4 m), the central hall and other levels is by stair, escalator and lift. A system of ramps provides official vehicles with access to the platforms when meeting visiting delegations, and taxis and private cars with access to the concourse-level car park.

The framework of the transparent roof reproduces, on a massive scale, the latticed structure of the walls in a traditional Kazakh yurt. An enormous arch towers over the station and the roads leading to it, highlighting the grand scale of Astana and its vast expanses. Under the vaults of the arch there is a single, unified space, designed to be easily navigated by users of the station.

Astana, Kazakhstan

CLIENT: Administration of Astana and
National Company Kazakhstan Temir Zholy
DESIGN: 2010 (1st place in international competition)
REALIZATION: N/A
TOTAL AREA: 57,510 sq m (station building: 33,670 sq m;
commercial building: 23,840 sq m)

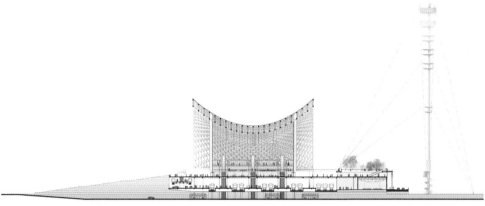

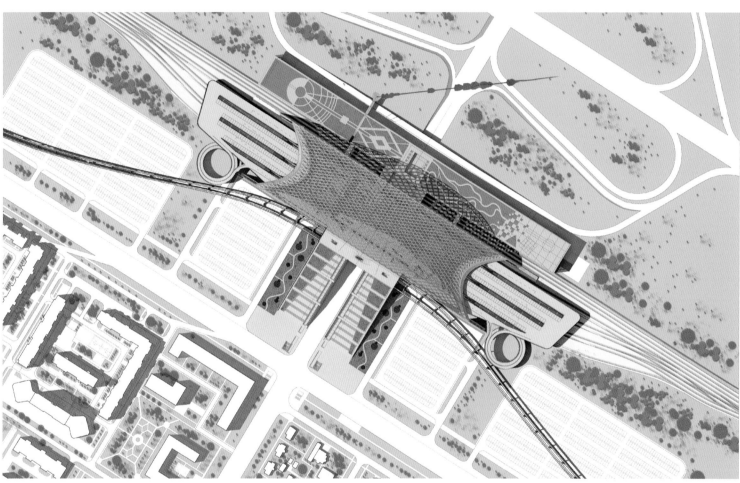

ABOVE
Some of the inspirations for the design
of the station roof.

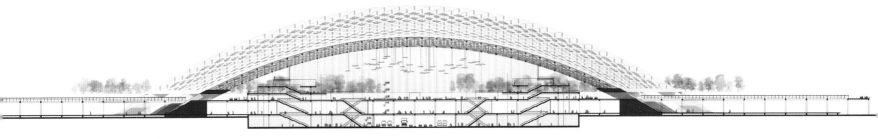

ABOVE
Longitudinal cross-section.

ABOVE
Longitudinal cross-section.

RIGHT
Plan of the station at +4.2 m.

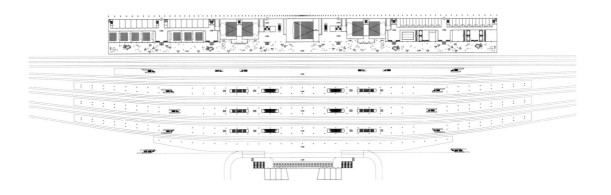

RIGHT
Plan of the station at +12 m.

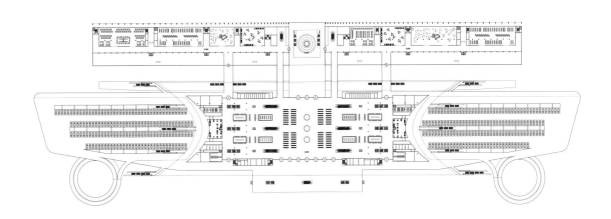

RIGHT
Roof plan.

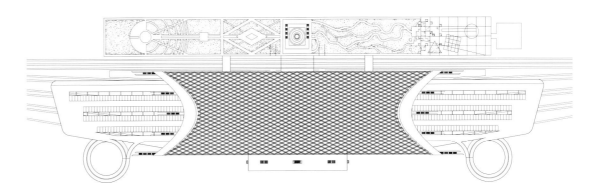

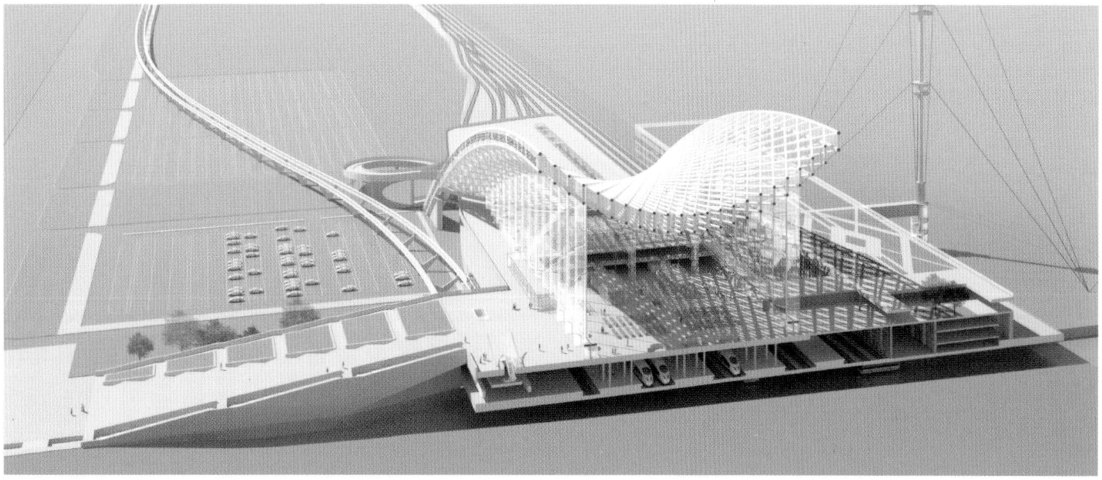

LEFT
Three-dimensional cross-section.

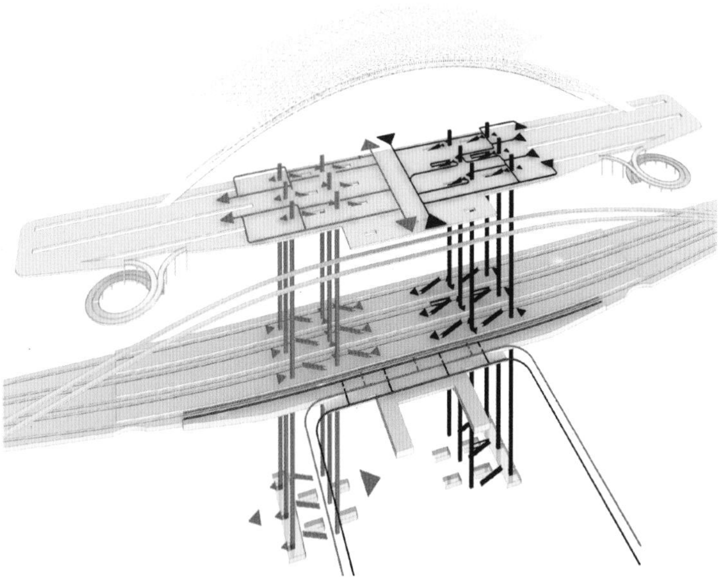

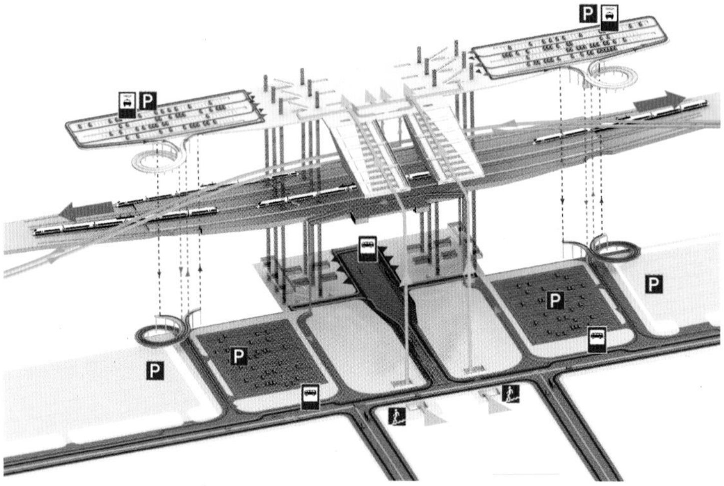

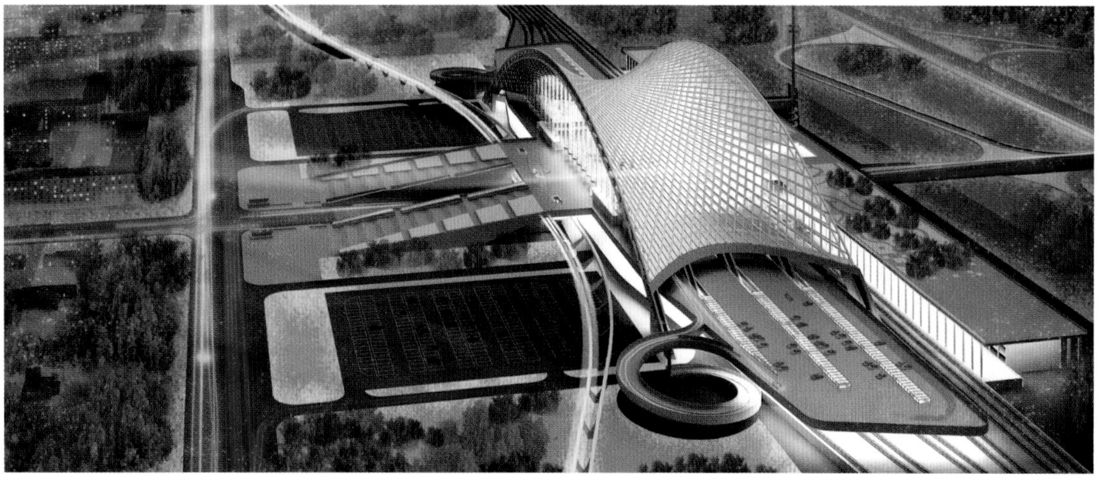

ABOVE, LEFT AND RIGHT
Diagrams showing the movement of passengers between the various parts of the station.

LEFT
The station complex viewed from above.

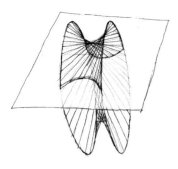

ABOVE
The shape of the roof is formed from a section of a hyperboloid.

RIGHT
Detail of the main façade.

RIGHT, BOTTOM
Interior of the central hall.

BELOW
Concept sketch for the roof.

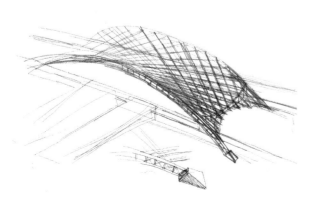

19

PALACE OF SCHOOLCHILDREN

The Palace of Schoolchildren in Astana is the largest educational and cultural centre for young people in the whole of the former USSR. The four-storey building comprises 840 different facilities, including a swimming pool, an ice rink, gyms, track-and-field facilities, a basketball court, a martial arts arena, a theatre, a planetarium, and art and music classrooms. Some ten thousand schoolchildren aged between seven and eighteen attend 109 clubs and 603 hobby groups here.

The architecture of the palace is a result of a dialogue with the traditional culture and architecture of the region, as illustrated by the project's slogan: 'Khan Shanyrak' (Shelter for Youth Creativity). The *shanyrak* is the circular wooden structure that crowns a Kazakh yurt, with an opening in the centre above the fireplace. This vital, even sacred element of a traditional Kazakh dwelling is reinterpreted in the palace as an opening through which light pours into the building's central atrium, the Forum. The main public and ceremonial space in the complex, the Forum is located in a circular area measuring 8 m in height and 156 m in diameter, home to the various clubs and groups.

In addition to the Forum, the circular area encompasses stepped compositions of rectangular 'boxes', each containing one of the palace's facilities. The boxes are placed one on top of the other like *shabadany* (felt suitcases), a feature of the nomadic lifestyle and the most important item of decoration in yurt interiors. In the palace, all the boxes have double-layered façades with structural glazing. The glass screens are embellished with nine different traditional Kazakh patterns.

5 Prospekt Bauyrzhana Momyshuly, Astana, Kazakhstan

CLIENT: NAK Kazatomprom
DESIGN: 2010
REALIZATION: 2011
GROSS FLOOR AREA: 40,500 sq m

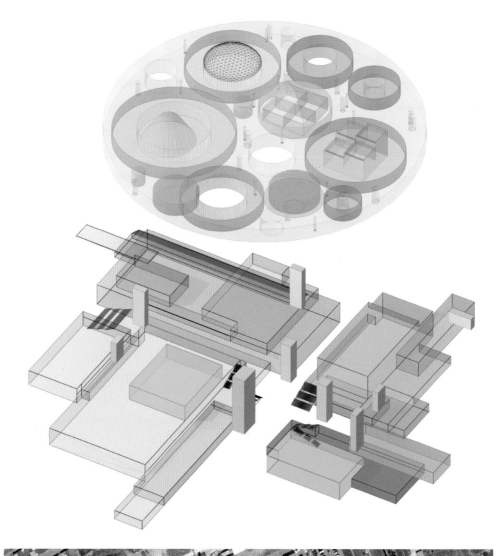

Eco-biological activities
Dance classes
Art facilities
Science and technical facilities
Human sciences
Auditorium
Music classes
Planetarium
Recreation
Theatre
Multipurpose hall
Sports hall
Media/IT centre
Dining hall
Museum/exhibition hall

ABOVE
A traditional Kazakh drawing, incorporating the circular form of the yurt.

RIGHT
View of the stairway and skylight in the central atrium.

OPPOSITE, LEFT
The construction of a yurt, a traditional Kazakh dwelling.

OPPOSITE, TOP RIGHT
Diagram showing the different facilities housed within the palace (see also key, above).

OPPOSITE, BOTTOM RIGHT
Aeriel view of the building and surrounding area.

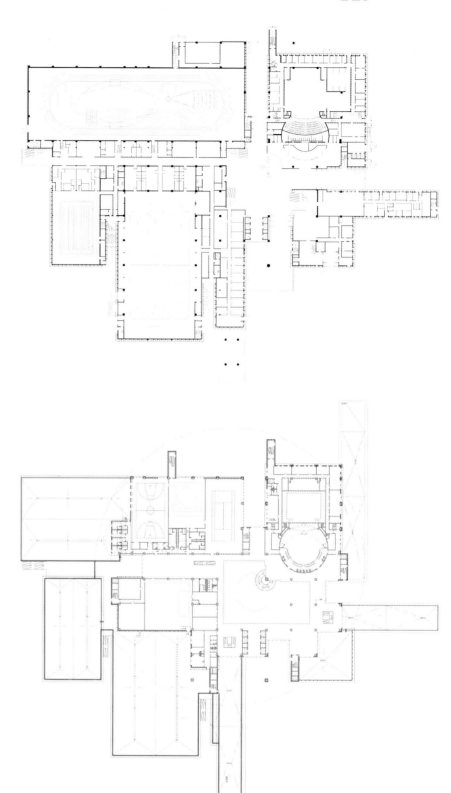

ABOVE, TOP
First-floor plan.

ABOVE
Second-floor plan.

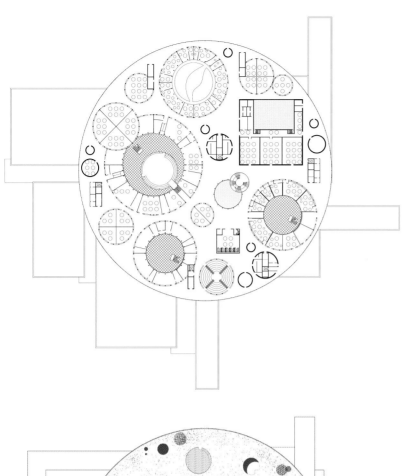

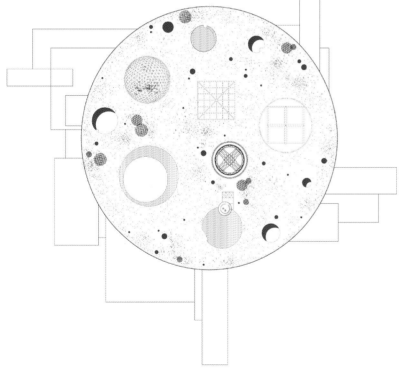

Fourth-floor plan.

Roof plan.

ABOVE
Views of some of the recreational
and educational facilities, including the
winter garden.

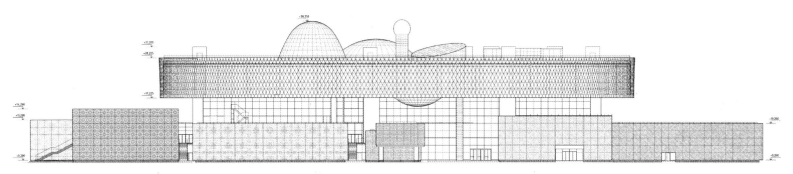

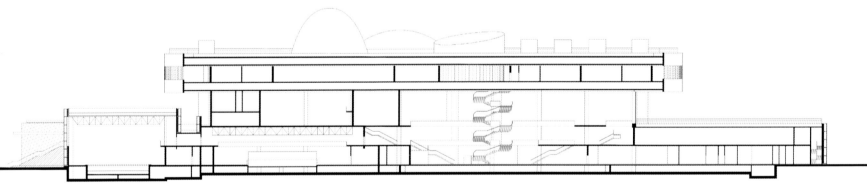

ABOVE, TOP, AND OPPOSITE, BOTTOM
Views of the palace at night.

ABOVE
Cross-section of the forum and
planetarium.

188   STUDIO 44

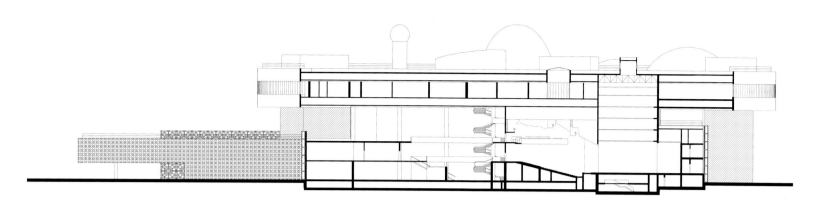

Cross-section of the theatre.

Interior of the central atrium,
also known as the Forum.

20

ZHASTAR YOUTH PALACE

Zhastar Youth Palace is a socially significant project. It is aimed at providing young people with opportunities to enjoy culture in their spare time, as well as at promoting positive values and a healthy lifestyle. The composition of the building is uniquely diverse. A concert hall and a multiplex, a music and dance club, a film studio, a discussion club and a registry office, a media library and a children's centre – all these facilities are packed within a 65 × 65 × 65-m cubic shell.

A conglomeration of volumes of different shapes and sizes can be seen through the transparent walls of the cube. Each volume contains one of the building's facilities, and stands out from the others by means of the colour and texture of its finish.

The volumes are linked in a way that encourages people who have different hobbies to socialize in a single atrium space.

Beneath the building, which is raised 5 m above ground level, is the Youth Forum, where major events are held. The palace adjoins a sports centre to the north, and an open-air amphitheatre to the south.

Zhastar is aligned with a pedestrian boulevard that runs for 2.7 km and was conceived as means of connecting a variety of different locations, covering all ages and social groups, within the city. One section of the boulevard – a promenade built at a height of 5 m – passes over Prospekt Respubliki and leads directly to the palace.

34 Prospekt Respubliki, Astana, Kazakhstan

CLIENT: Administration of Astana
DESIGN: 2012 (1st place in international competition)
REALIZATION: N/A
TOTAL AREA: 42,850 sq m

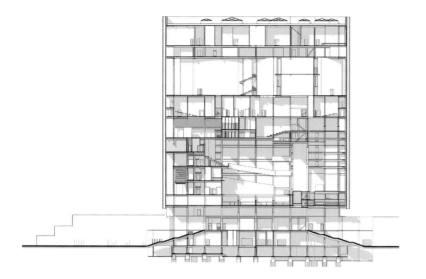

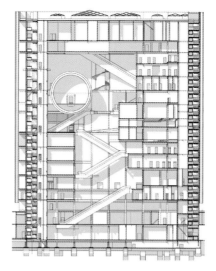

ABOVE, LEFT AND RIGHT
Cross-sections of the cubic part of the building.

BELOW
Diagram showing the different parts of the palace and how they fit together to form a whole.

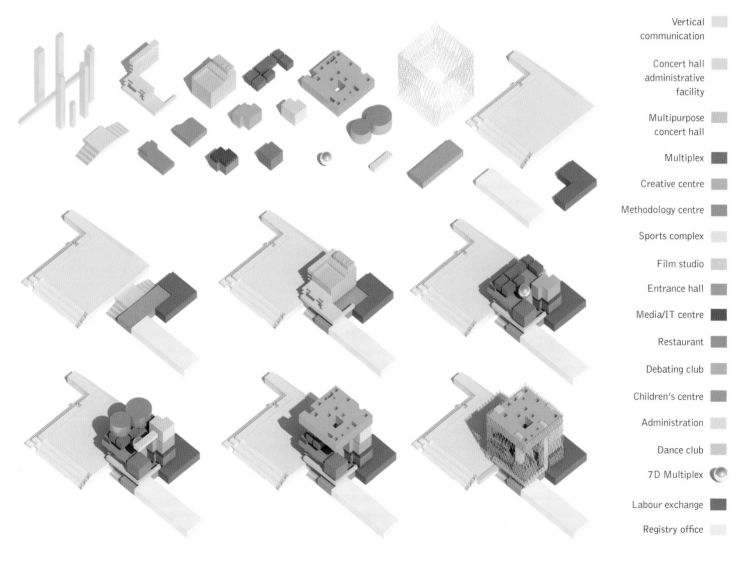

Vertical communication

Concert hall administrative facility

Multipurpose concert hall

Multiplex

Creative centre

Methodology centre

Sports complex

Film studio

Entrance hall

Media/IT centre

Restaurant

Debating club

Children's centre

Administration

Dance club

7D Multiplex

Labour exchange

Registry office

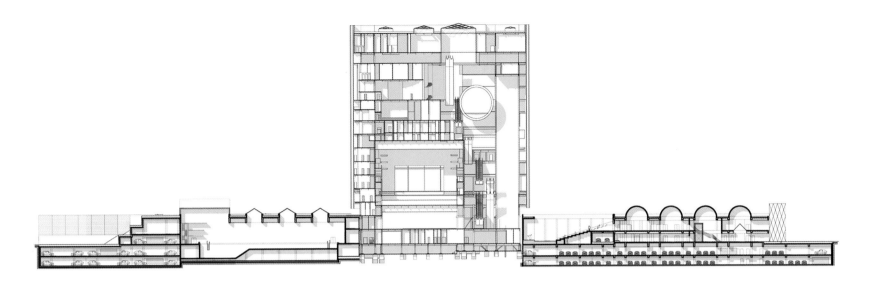

ABOVE
Longitudinal cross-section of the entire building.

LEFT
Plan of the building at ground-floor level.

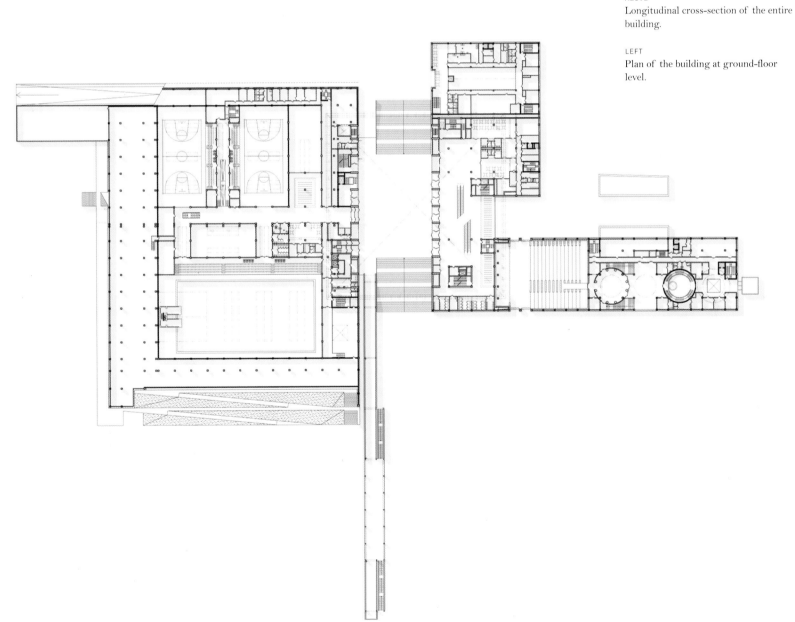

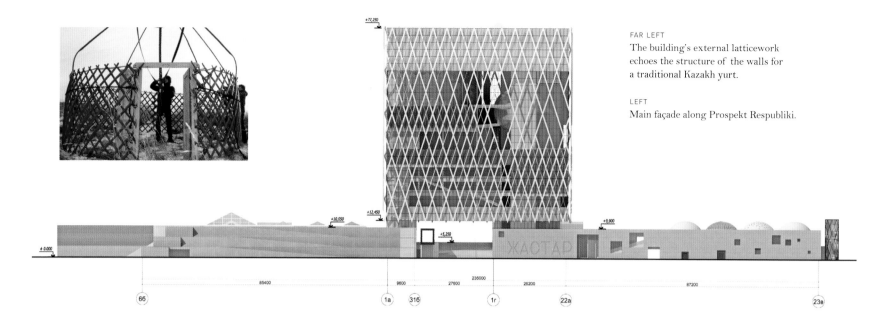

FAR LEFT
The building's external latticework
echoes the structure of the walls for
a traditional Kazakh yurt.

LEFT
Main façade along Prospekt Respubliki.

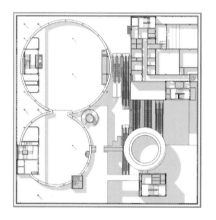

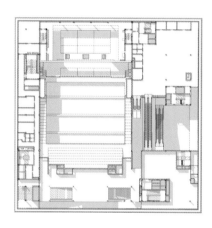

FAR LEFT
Floor plan at +50.9 m.

LEFT
Floor plan at +29.3 m.

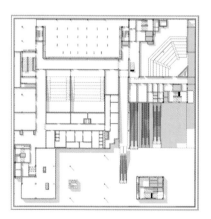

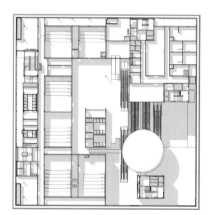

FAR LEFT
Floor plan at +38.9 m.

LEFT
Floor plan at +43.7 m.

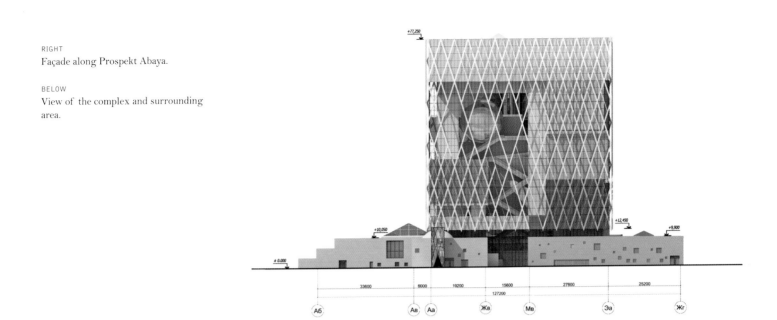

LEFT
Views of the interior of Zhastar
Youth Palace.

ABOVE
View of the complex from Prospekt
Respubliki.

ZHASTAR YOUTH PALACE

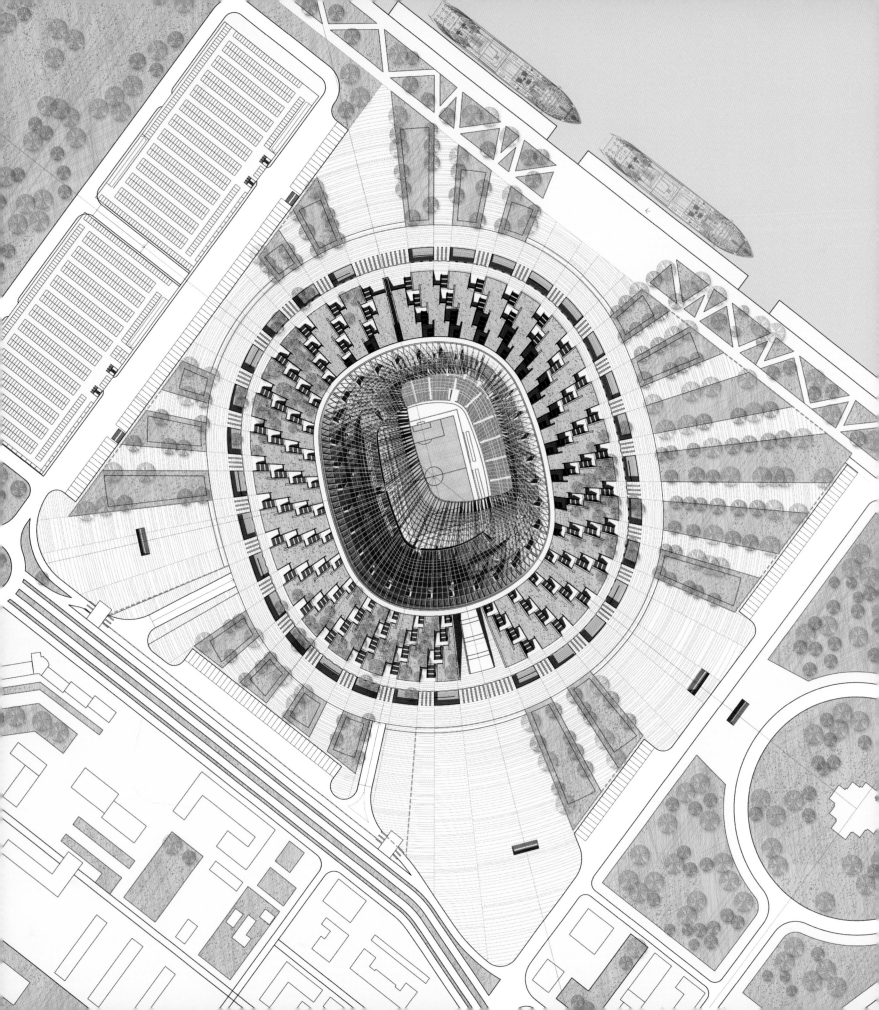

21

FOOTBALL STADIUM FOR 2018 FIFA WORLD CUP

With a capacity of 42,000, the stadium is designed in the form of a green hill crowned with the snow-white bowl of the upper stands. At the heart of the hill is the football pitch, with three tiers of seating for 33,000 spectators.

The stadium is surrounded by auxiliary facilities. Along the outer contour of the structure they form a stepped composition, which, as a result of filling the terrace steps with topsoil, is in the shape of a gently sloping hill.

On the landscaped slopes of the hill, a series of staircases provide access to the stands. With thirty staircases to each of the five spectator zones, there are 150 entranceways in total, allowing for the optimum movement of people and reducing to a minimum the time required to fill the stadium or evacuate it in the case of an emergency. In addition to the staircases, there are lifts and escalators in the main entrance zone, where the hill ceremoniously 'opens out'.

The upper stands seat 9,000, giving the stadium the total capacity it needs in order to function as a venue for the 2018 World Cup. The bowl of upper stands is raised 3 m above the top of the hill on pylons, which create the impression that the bowl is hovering in mid-air. Following the World Cup, the upper stands may be dismantled and reassembled as and when required. Without them, the stadium begins to acquire a raised relief or mound effect. It fits in very naturally at the spot where the Volga and Oka rivers converge.

Nizhny Novgorod, Russia

CLIENT: N/A (initiative of Studio 44)
DESIGN: 2012
REALIZATION: N/A
GROSS FLOOR AREA: 93,360 sq m

Design for the S. M. Kirov Stadium by
Alexander Nikolsky, 1932.

The Chkalov Staircase in Nizhny
Novgorod.

The upper stands of the stadium can be
dismantled, to be used at a later date.

Axonometric cross-section.

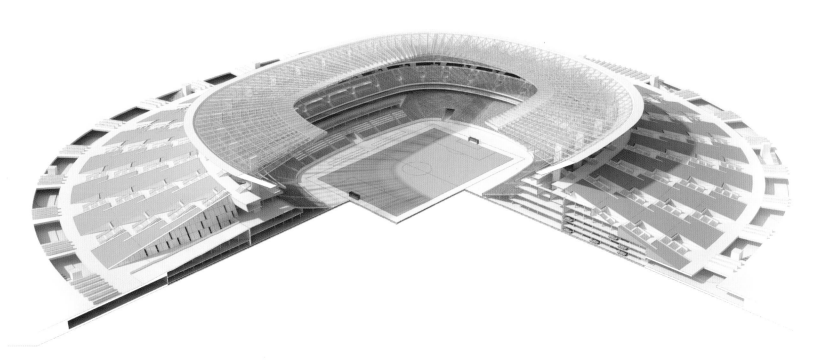

ABOVE
Cross-section.

RIGHT
Floor plans at 0.0 m (top left), +10 m
(top right), +19 m (bottom left) and
+24 m (bottom right).

ABOVE, TOP
View from the stadium towards the Volga River.

ABOVE, LEFT AND RIGHT
Concept sketches for the stadium hill, showing the landscaping and the staircases providing access to the stands.

ABOVE
Concept sketch of the entire stadium.

RIGHT AND BELOW
A total of 150 staircases provide access
to the stands.

22

OLYMPIC PARK RAILWAY STATION

Olympic Park railway station was envisaged as the main land gateway to the 22nd Winter Olympics in Sochi. From here, crowds of people – 10,000 at peak hours – set off for the various Olympic venues. The design of the station is derived from the trajectory of this movement, both obeying and managing it. The canopies over the platforms merge smoothly into the roof, which towers proudly above the central area before flowing smoothly downwards, as if ushering the crowds of visitors towards the Olympic Park.

The design of the station brings to mind the folds of a mountain or the waves of an ocean. Above all, however, the station resembles a bird with outspread wings – a bird with a spine, a skeleton that gradually gets thinner and thinner, skin, and even wing flaps. This avian morphology brings the station close to bionic architecture.

The station stands on the edge of a 6-m ledge, which allowed the station square to be built over two levels: the upper for pedestrians and the lower for vehicles (including a bus station).

The internal structure of the station is multi-levelled and staggered. Commuter facilities are mainly located in the space beneath the platforms, while the passenger area for long-distance trains is a concourse located on a level above the tracks. This area is designed as a single, flowing space with various levels from which – be it the lobby, the restaurant or the central hall – a panoramic view of the Olympic Park and its venues opens up.

Sochi, Russia

CLIENT: Russian Railways, Directorate for Renovation and Construction
DESIGN: 2010–12
REALIZATION: 2011–13
GROSS FLOOR AREA: 17,200 sq m

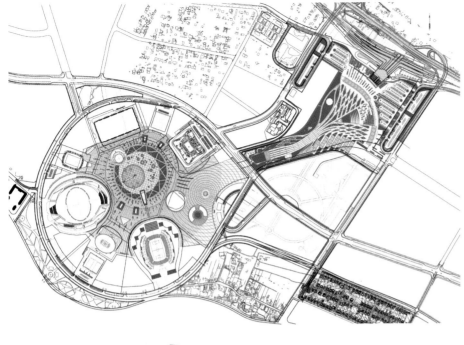

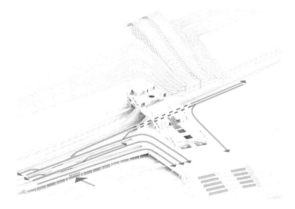

ABOVE, TOP
Map showing the location of the station in relation to the Olympic Park.

ABOVE
Concept sketch for the station.

ABOVE
From top: the main inspiration for the station's design; the transparent roof structure; diagram showing passenger movement.

OPPOSITE, TOP
Mock-up of the station, viewed from above.

OPPOSITE, BOTTOM
A bird's-eye view of the station during the construction process.

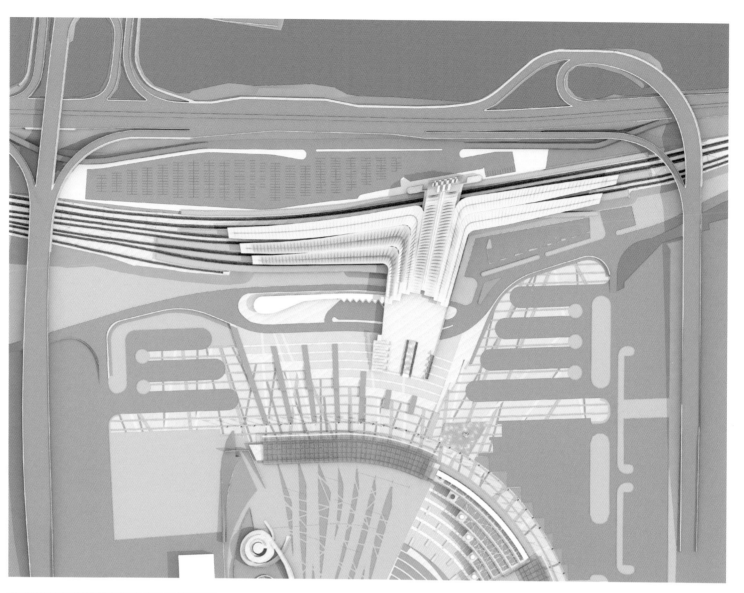

ABOVE
Main façade.

ABOVE
Various levels of the station open up to views of the Olympic venues.

ABOVE, RIGHT
View of the station with the Olympic Park in the background.

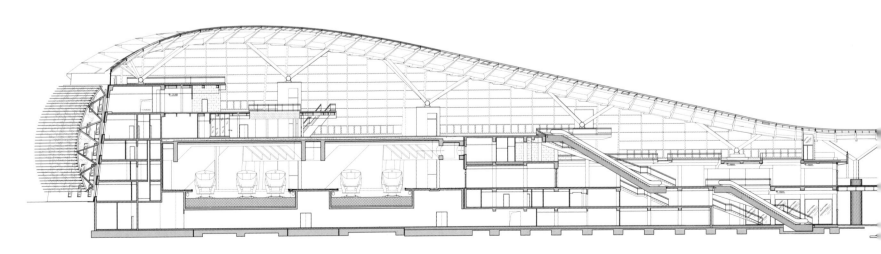

STUDIO 44

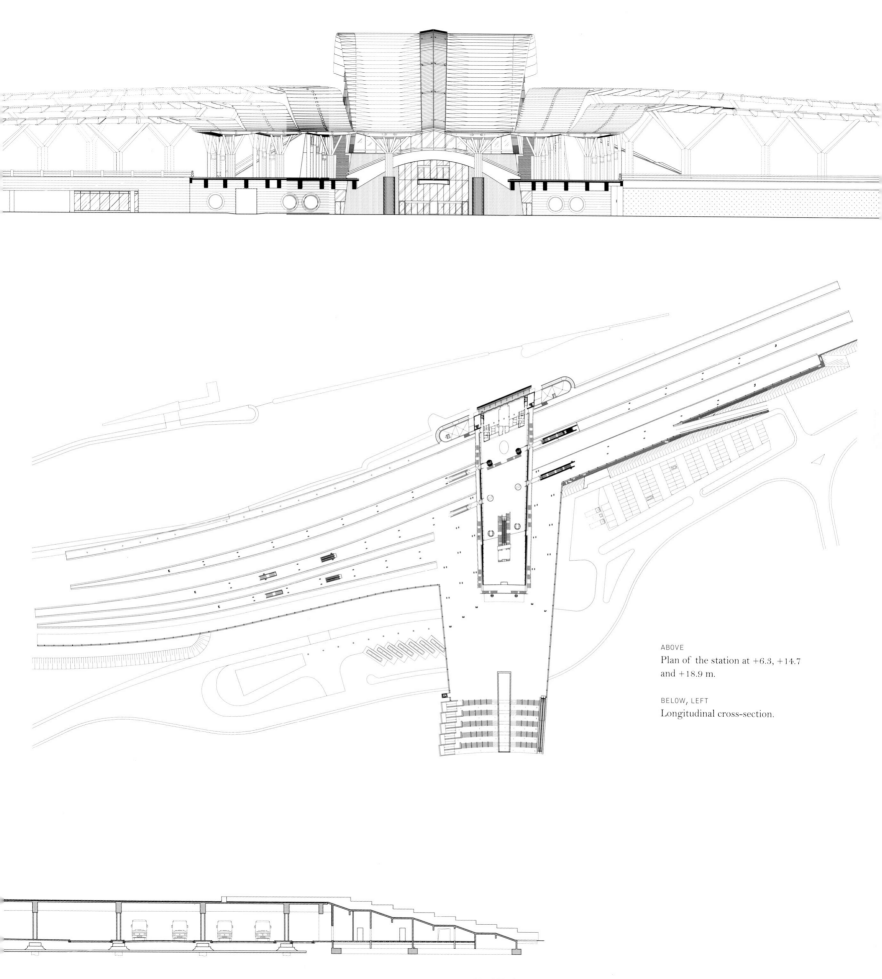

ABOVE
Plan of the station at +6.3, +14.7 and +18.9 m.

BELOW, LEFT
Longitudinal cross-section.

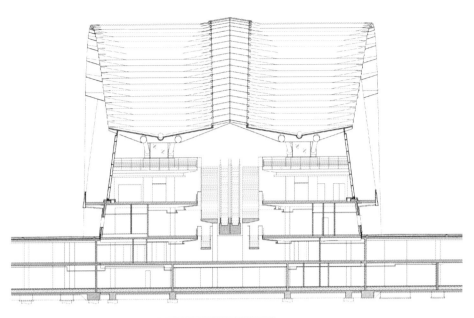

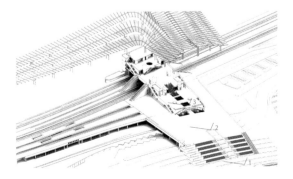

ABOVE
Latitudinal cross-section.

LEFT
From top: station interior; the main entrance to the building; stairs with water feature; diagram showing the different levels of the station.

RIGHT
The passenger hall for intercity trains.

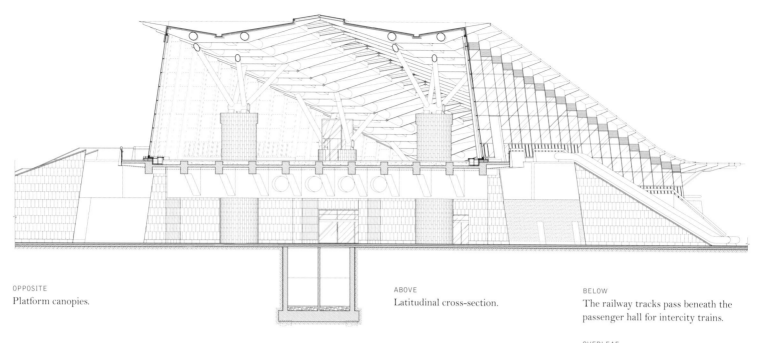

OPPOSITE
Platform canopies.

ABOVE
Latitudinal cross-section.

BELOW
The railway tracks pass beneath the passenger hall for intercity trains.

OVERLEAF
The station in its mountainous setting.

23

TSAR'S GARDEN
HOTEL COMPLEX

The complex is located in Zamoskvorechye District, where a vast Tsar's Garden, the pride of Russia's capital city, could be found between the fifteenth and seventeenth centuries. An interesting feature of seventeenth-century Russian architecture were the 'upper gardens' established on the roofs of Moscow buildings. Both of these historical phenomena, resonating as they do with the modern concept of eco-friendly living, served as reference points for the design of the current project.

Between the two blocks of the complex – one residential, the other commercial – is a landscaped garden. Gently sloping downwards towards Sofiyskaya Embankment, the garden resembles an amphitheatre facing the Moskva River and the walls of the Kremlin. The accessible roof areas on both blocks are conceived as green viewing areas.

On the roof of the commercial block, there is a regular garden. On the residential block, the penthouse terraces have been transformed into hanging gardens, surrounded by latticed railings covered in climbing plants.

The lattice motif continues on the façade of the residential block, where the walls are made up of two layers: a lace-like stone shell with transparent volumes within. The ornament of the outer layer reminds one of garden fences and pergolas.

In fact, the design of the façade of the residential block incorporates a whole series of references: the carved patterns of mediaeval Moscow, the decorative shells of Muscovite baroque and the architectural experimentation of the 1920s (in particular, Ivan Zholtovsky's pavilions at the All-Russian Agricultural Exhibition, 1923). In any case, the latticed pattern determines the rhythm and structure of the façade, visually separating the very long building into several sections.

36/10 Sofiyskaya Embankment, Central Administrative District, Moscow, Russia

CLIENT: Midland Development
DESIGN: 2013 (1st place in closed, regional competition)
REALIZATION: N/A
TOTAL AREA: 78,038 sq m

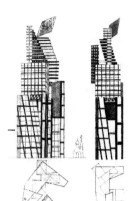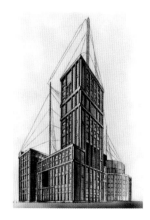

LEFT
Architectural inspirations for the hotel complex (from left): the Supreme National Economic Committee building, Moscow (Vladimir Krinsky, 1922–3); the Palace of Labour, Moscow (Vesnin brothers, 1923); detail of Vasily Blazhenov Church, Moscow (Postnik Yakovlev, 1561); entrance pavilion, All-Russian Agricultural Exhibition, Moscow (Ivan Zholtovsky, 1923).

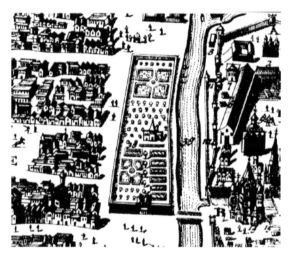

FAR LEFT
Seventeenth-century view of the Tsar's Garden, Zamoskvorechye District. From a detailed plan of Moscow by A. Olearia, 1656.

LEFT
Location of the hotel complex in relation to the site of the Tsar's Garden.

LEFT
General plan.

OPPOSITE, TOP
Street view of the complex with Bolshoy Moscovoretsky Bridge in the foreground.

OPPOSITE, BOTTOM
Detail of the façade of the residential block.

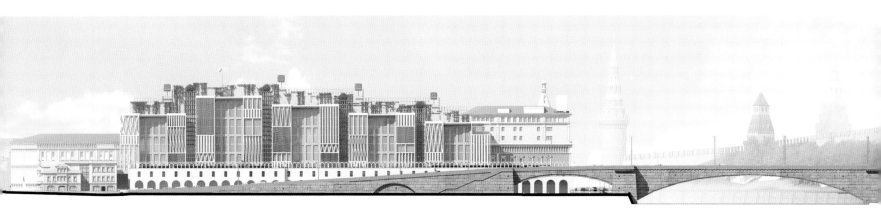

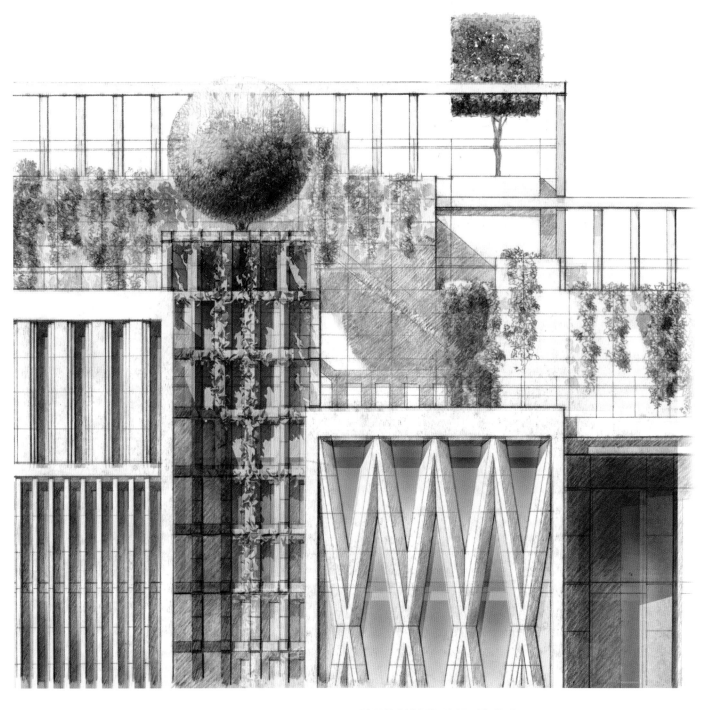

TSAR'S GARDEN HOTEL COMPLEX

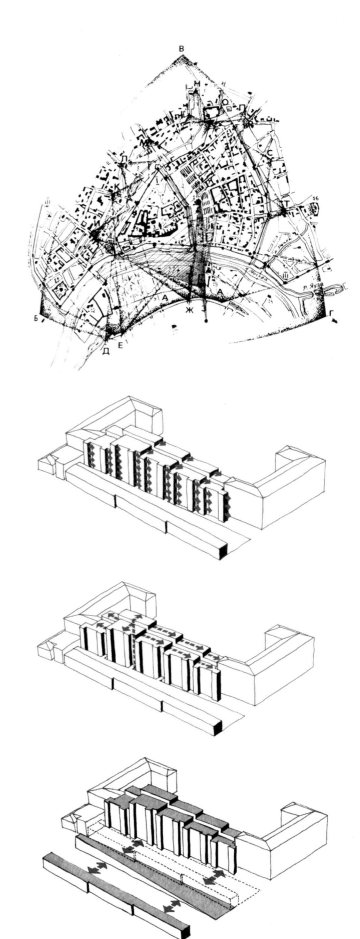

OPPOSITE, TOP LEFT
Design sketch.

OPPOSITE, BOTTOM LEFT
The landscaped garden between the residential and commercial blocks.

OPPOSITE, TOP RIGHT
Diagram of panoramic views of the centre of Moscow.

OPPOSITE, BOTTOM RIGHT
From top: optimization scheme for various features of the residential block; organizational scheme for access to the roof terraces; scheme for the green areas of the complex.

RIGHT
View from one of the 'upper gardens' on the roof of the residential block.

BELOW
View of the complex from the roof of the Balchug Kempinsky hotel on Bolshoy Moskvoretsky Bridge.

View of the complex from Bolshoy
Moskoversky Bridge.

STUDIO 44

24

SCIENCE AND TECHNOLOGY MUSEUM

The construction of the Science and Technology Museum is part of a state programme aimed at transforming the university town of Tomsk into the largest scientific and educational centre in Western Siberia.

The design of the museum redefines and develops the building traditions of Tomsk, deservedly considered a heritage area for Russian wooden architecture. In particular, the museum's appearance alludes to the wooden fortress around which the city grew up in the seventeenth century.

The building is 225 m long and 35 m wide, and runs parallel to the banks of the Tom River. Dominating the two-storey, gabled-roof structure are five mighty 'towers', each in the shape of an archetypal form: hexagon, square, circle, cross and octagon. The museum's display areas are located inside these towers. A sixth tower serves as a "look-out post", with three levels of viewing platforms.

On the first floor of the museum, galleries accessible by stairs from the ground floor run around the outside of the building. In sixteenth- and seventeenth-century Russian architecture, similar galleries around churches or palaces were known as *gulbishche*. Like their predecessors, the museum's *gulbishche* act as public spaces, places to socialize, relax and enjoy the surrounding views.

The museum will be built in Tatarskaya Sloboda, an area of Tomsk famous for its wooden houses lavishly decorated in the Eastern style. However, the design of the museum will not simply replicate such decoration, and there is much from the art of Russian wooden architecture in the project. In fact, based on the innovations of constructivism in the 1920s, its aim is to show that the neat geometric plan of its wooden frame can coexist with the beautiful pattern-work of carved ornaments.

Tomsk, Russia

CLIENT: Tomsk State University of Architecture and Construction
DESIGN: 2014 (1st place in international competition)
REALIZATION: Work in progress
TOTAL AREA: 11,958 sq m

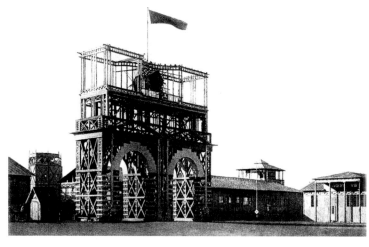

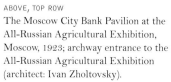

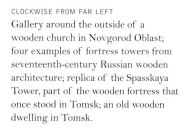

The Moscow City Bank Pavilion at the All-Russian Agricultural Exhibition, Moscow, 1923; archway entrance to the All-Russian Agricultural Exhibition (architect: Ivan Zholtovsky).

Triumphal arch, erected in 1891, to mark the visit of Tsetsarevich Nikolai Alexandrovich to Tomsk; Makhorka Pavilion at the All-Russian Agricultural Exhibition (architect: Konstantin Melnikhov).

Gallery around the outside of a wooden church in Novgorod Oblast; four examples of fortress towers from seventeenth-century Russian wooden architecture; replica of the Spasskaya Tower, part of the wooden fortress that once stood in Tomsk; an old wooden dwelling in Tomsk.

ABOVE
Bird's-eye view of the museum, with
the Tom River on the right.

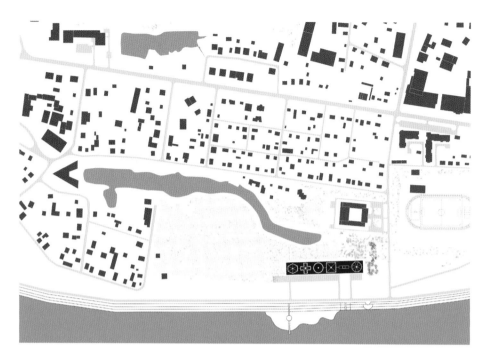

LEFT
Area map.

BELOW
Site plan.

OPPOSITE, TOP
View of the museum from the
Tom River.

OPPOSITE, BOTTOM
Floor plans at 0 m, +4.5 m (the
main exhibition level) and +8 m.

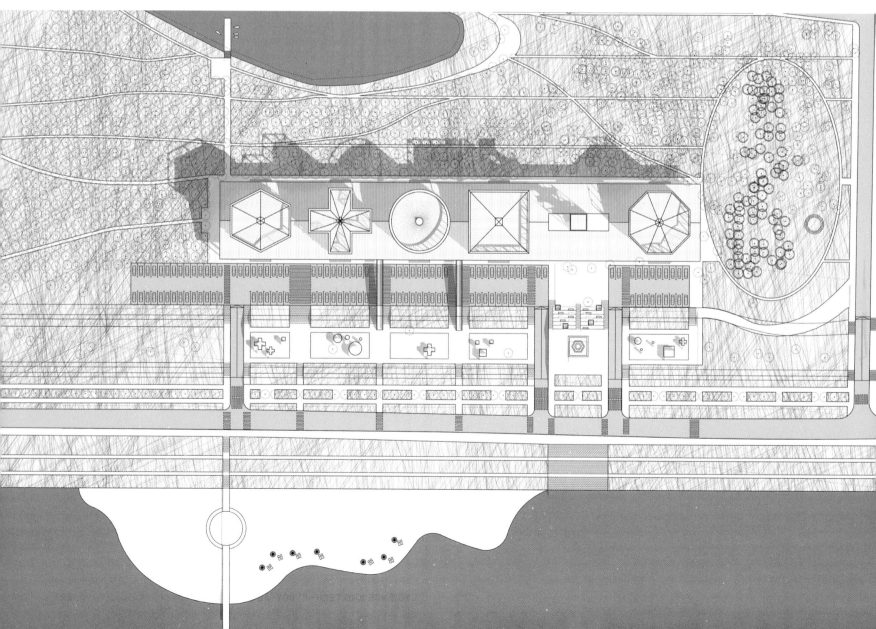

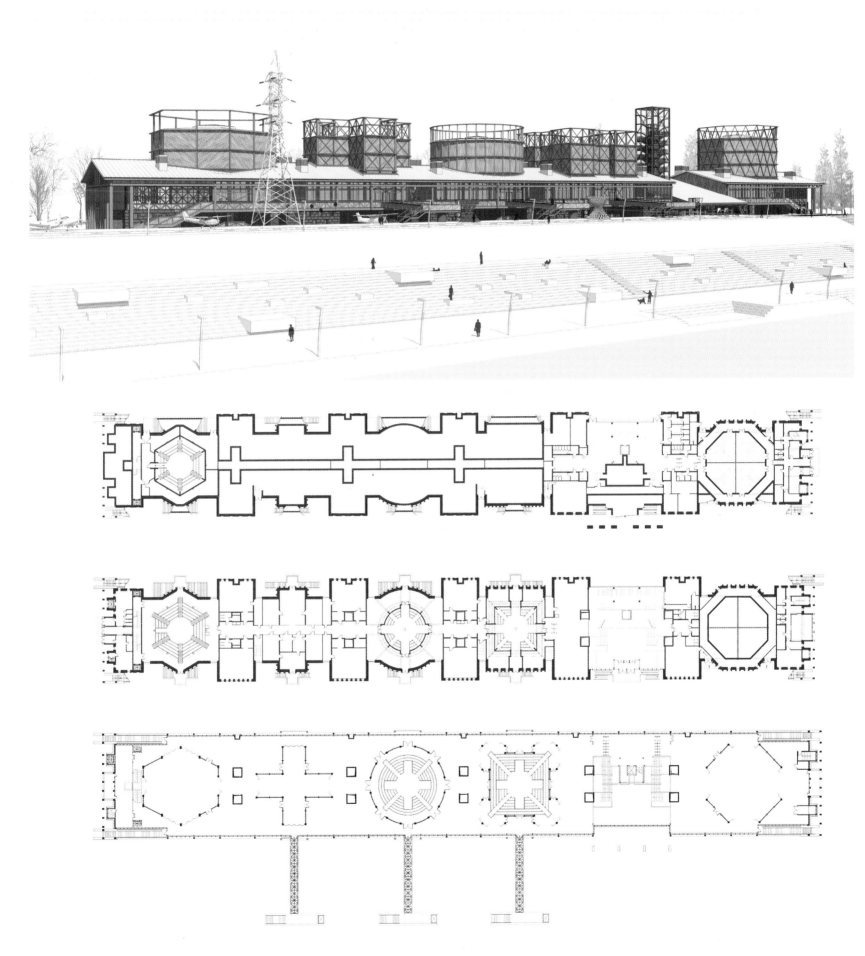

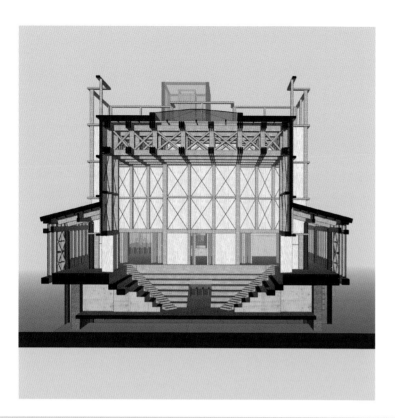

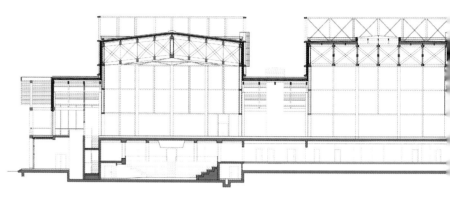

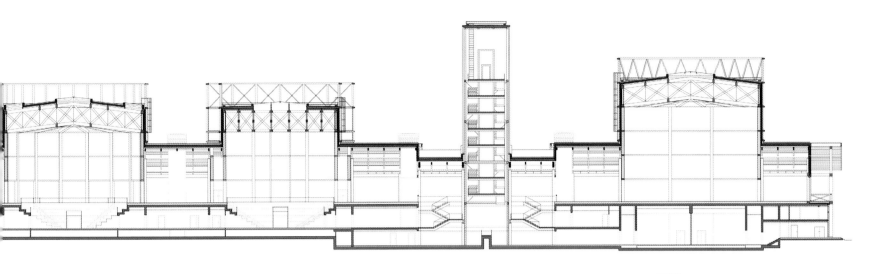

BELOW
Interior of the square tower.

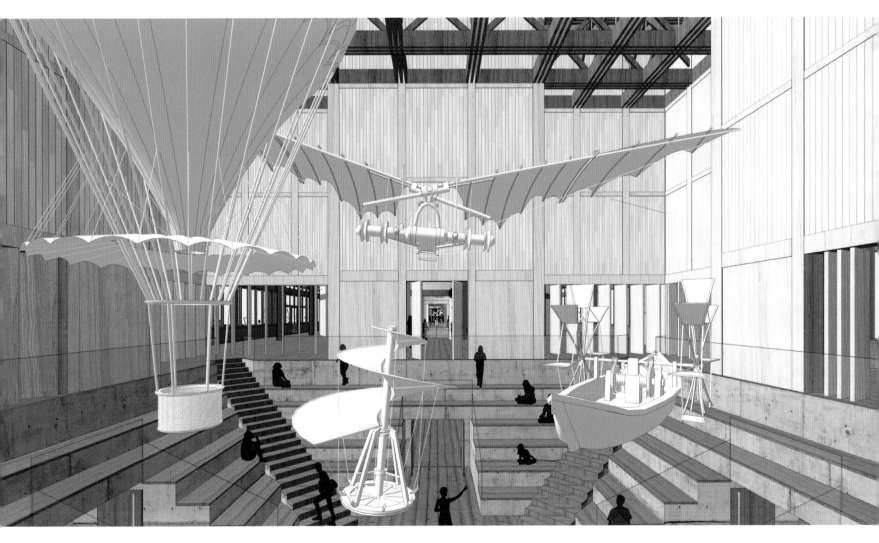

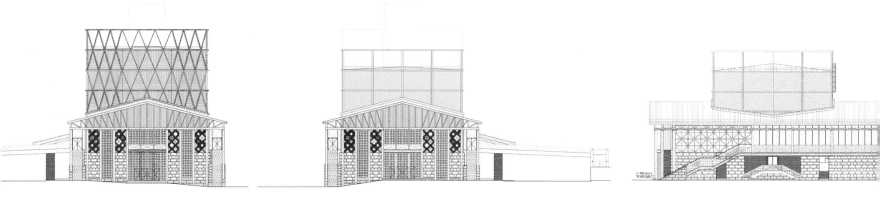

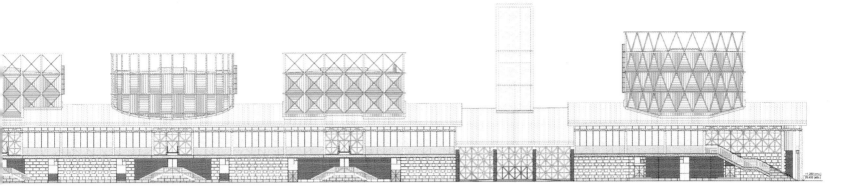

ABOVE
Side and main façades.

OPPOSITE, BOTTOM
View of one side of the building.

BELOW
The external gallery on the first floor, with the wooden gangways that connect the museum to the riverbank.

View of the museum from the
riverside promenade.

25

CAMPUS OF GRADUATE SCHOOL OF MANAGEMENT, ST PETERSBURG UNIVERSITY

Revitalization of a 19th-century imperial residence

St Petersburg University's Graduate School of Management is fully integrated into the global educational system, holding a unique portfolio of educational and research programmes. The 'Russian Berkeley', as it is known, can accommodate 1,800 students and 150 lecturers.

The site of the school's suburban campus is Mikhailovskaya Dacha, a summer residence of Mikhail Nikolaevich, the fourth son of Tsar Nicholas I of Russia. The building programme for the campus was twofold: the restoration and conversion of architectural monuments to meet the needs of a twenty-first-century business school, and the construction of new buildings.

While designing an environment for the educational activities of 1,400 students in what used to be a stables block (1861, designed by Harold Bosse), Studio 44 attempted to recreate the unique structure of the building, its axial hierarchy and its inner logic. Thus, the main cour d'honneur was saved from new construction, with the 450-seat auditorium that was planned for this location being moved to a semi-underground elliptical volume just beyond the stables block. An open cloister flows into the roofed recreation lounge known as the Forum, and together they form a series of spaces for socializing.

One of the new buildings, the student cafeteria and club, is located at the intersection of five main thoroughfares. This fact determined the shape of the building and explains the five entrances of equal importance. The lower level contains the dining hall. From here, one can go up to the terraces that spiral around the core of the building – the assembly hall. This configuration creates a centripetal effect, helping to bring people closer together. The spiral motif is continued in the roof of the building, which rises gradually from the periphery towards the centre. The transparent walls appear to dissolve the entire structure in the surrounding landscape.

109 Sankt-Peterburgskoe Shosse, Petrodvortsovy District, St Petersburg, Russia

CLIENT: Russia Federal Agency for Education, St Petersburg University
DESIGN: 2007–12
REALIZATION: 2009–15
TOTAL AREA: 107,434 sq m (new buildings: 69,905 sq m; restored and converted buildings: 37,529 sq m)

LEFT
The eastern part of the campus, where the focus was on the restoration and adaptation of existing buildings.

LEFT
The eastern part of the campus, where the focus was on the restoration and adaptation of existing buildings.

LEFT, BOTTOM
The new-build part of the building programme was implemented in the western part of the campus.

ABOVE
Ideology of the restoration and adaptation of the Stable Building: intergration of new levels within the internal space of the building.

BELOW
Historical plan of the Stable Building, complete with dressage arena.

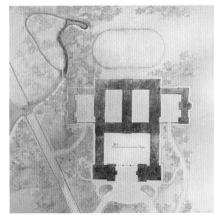

RIGHT
Views of the interior of the Stable
Building before restoration.

BELOW, LEFT
Ideology of the restoration and
adaptation of the Stable Building:
overlapping of nineteenth- and twenty-
first-century structural frameworks.

BELOW, RIGHT
Comparison of the functional
arrangement and axis hierarchies
of the Stable Building, before and
after restoration.

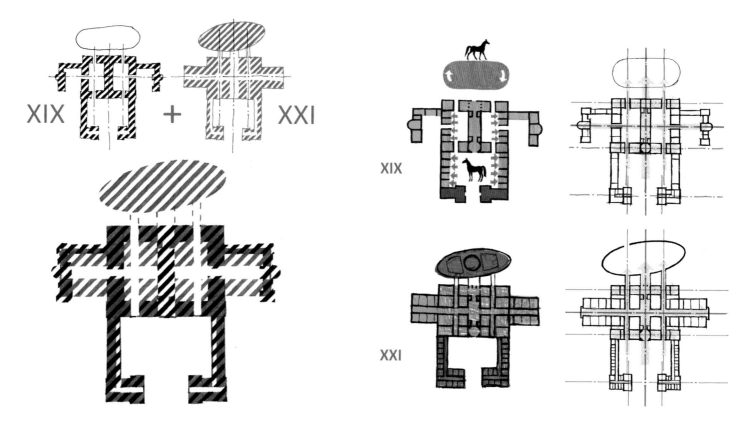

XIX + XXI

XIX

XXI

ABOVE
View of the main complex from
the north.

RIGHT
Second-floor plan.

BELOW
Cutaway model of the main complex.

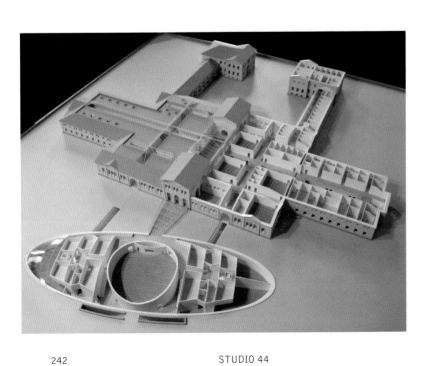

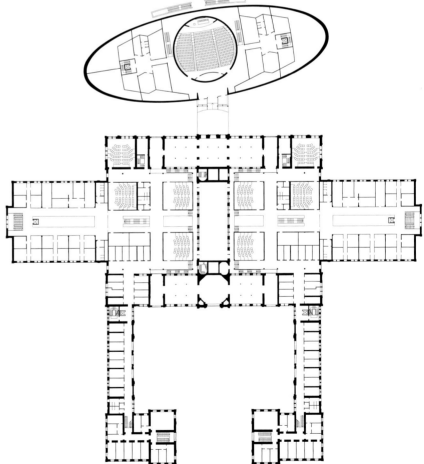

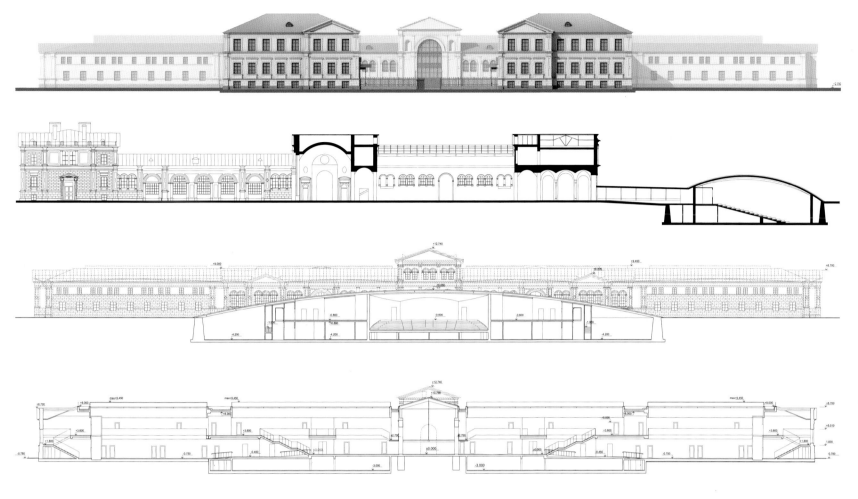

ABOVE
From top: northern façade, facing the
Finnish Peninsula; longitudinal cross-
section; cross-section of the attached
auditorium; cross-section showing the
lecture halls.

BELOW
View of the main complex from
the south.

Two of the lecture halls.

New stairwell in the main complex.

Entrance and reception area.

View of the Forum recreation
lounge from the entrance area.

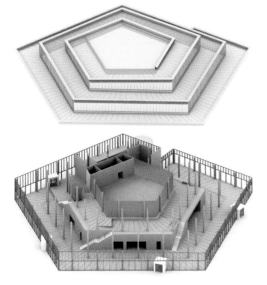

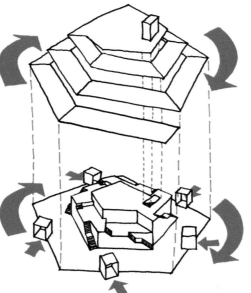

ABOVE
Bird's-eye view of the student cafeteria and club.

FAR LEFT
Axonometric model of the building.

LEFT
Conceptual design and layout of the student cafeteria and club.

ABOVE
External views of the student cafeteria and club.

RIGHT
Plan of the dining-hall level.

FAR RIGHT
Plan of the club-lounge level.

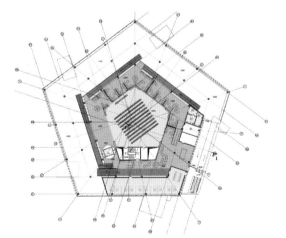

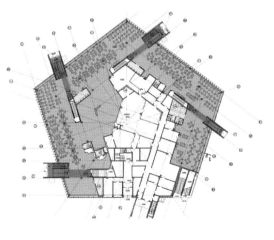

The transparent walls of the student cafeteria and club allow it to blend in with the landscape.

LEFT AND OPPOSITE
Interior of the dining hall on the ground floor.

26

BORIS EIFMAN
DANCE ACADEMY

Boris Eifman Dance Academy is a creative laboratory founded on the famous Russian choreographer's concept of modern dance – an experimental environment in which innovative methods of training international, twenty-first-century dancers are developed. About 60 per cent of the students are talented children who have lost their parents or come from at-risk families, and the academy provides them with an opportunity to acquire a prestigious profession and a stable position in society.

The academy comprises, to the north, a teaching block and, to the south, an accommodation block. Featuring a curved façade, the latter houses a hall of residence for 135 people and a medical centre. The former consists of a well-equipped sports centre with a swimming pool and gym, general education classrooms, two ballet classrooms and the academy's administrative offices.

The space between the teaching and accommodation blocks is designed as a covered atrium, with recreation lounges alongside several dance studios. The studios and lounges are liberally spread across various levels, connected by a clever system of stairs, lifts and galleries.

To give the academy as much light as possible, the walls of the recreation areas and dance studios are made of semi-transparent glass. In contrast to the light and airy interiors, traditional materials (brick and plaster) were used for the external façades. The restored façade of the former Assembly cinema (1913, F. Korzukhin) has become the academy's emblem. Added to the entrance recess at the front of the building – its main embellishment – is the name of the academy and a QR-code bas-relief with encoded quotations from famous dancers and choreographers on the art of dance.

2 Lizy Chaikinoy Street, St Petersburg, Russia

CLIENT: The Government of St Petersburg Construction Committee
DESIGN: 2008–10
REALIZATION: 2010–12
GROSS FLOOR AREA: 11,939 sq m

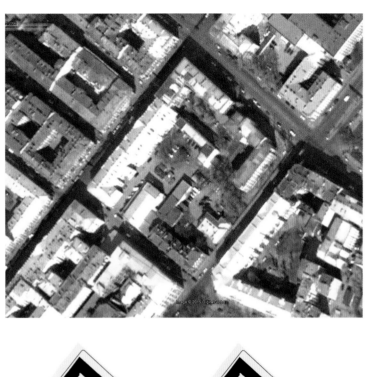

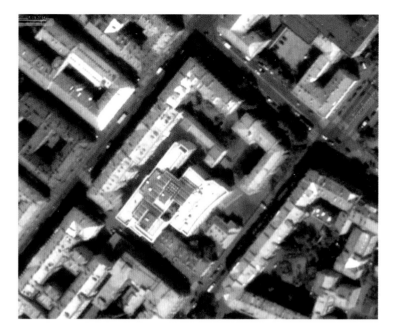

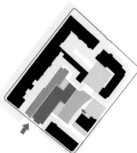

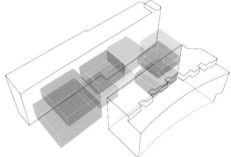

ABOVE, LEFT AND RIGHT
Aerial photographs of the site of the academy before and after construction.

FAR LEFT AND CENTRE
Integration of the academy with the surrounding residential block.

LEFT
Functional diagram of the building.

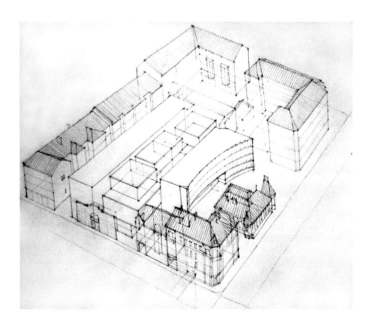

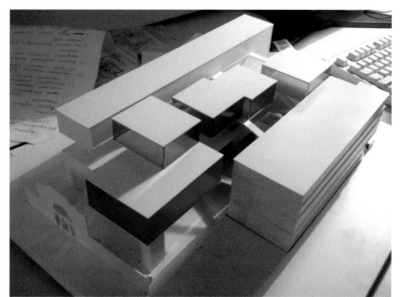

ABOVE, LEFT
Design sketch.

ABOVE
Working model.

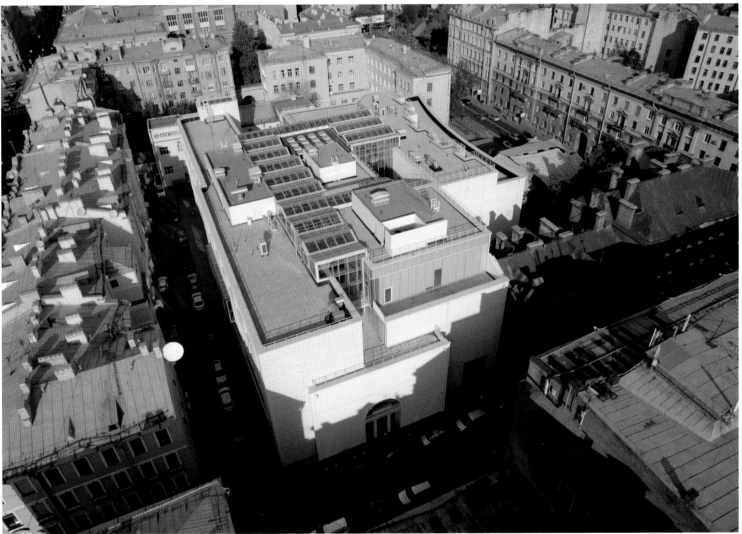

ABOVE, TOP
A selection of views of the
accommodation block.

ABOVE
Bird's-eye view of the whole complex.

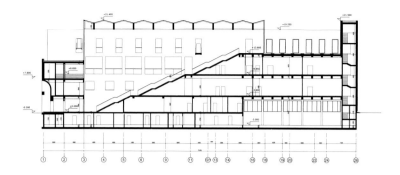

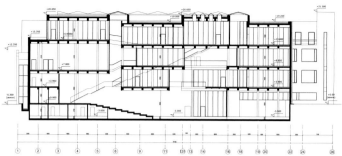

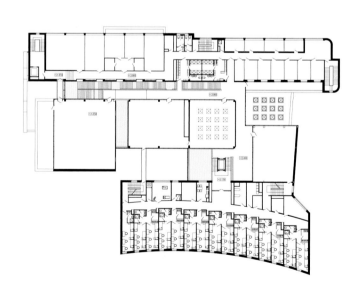

OPPOSITE, TOP ROW
Cross-section of the atrium and
of the rehearsal rooms.

OPPOSITE, CENTRE ROW
First- and second-floor plans.

OPPOSITE, BOTTOM ROW
Third- and fourth-floor plans.

THIS PAGE
Model of the academy.

STUDIO 44

LEFT
The main staircase in the atrium.

ABOVE
View of the atrium's interior.

BELOW AND RIGHT
Alternation of rehearsal rooms and
recreational spaces in the atrium.

OPPOSITE, TOP
Upper rehearsal rooms.

OPPOSITE, BOTTOM
Multilevel spaces in the atrium.

ABOVE AND RIGHT
Semi-transparent glass is used
throughout the atrium.

STUDIO 44

LEFT
External view of the rehearsal rooms.

BELOW
Rehearsal-room interiors.

ABOVE
Two of the rehearsal rooms seen from
the outside.

CITY CENTRES

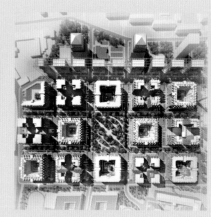

In parallel with the expansion in size and complexity of its architectural commissions, and its increasingly public character, Studio 44 is now taking on more and more projects on an urban scale. In each of its urban-planning projects, Studio 44 seeks to create a similar structural logic as can be found in its architectural commissions. The studio's most recent urban planning reflects an ambition, and capacity, to reconcile the new with the existing, taking the diversity and contradictions of the city into account, and accepting them as givens.

In the projects created ex novo, such as the idea for a coastal residential district in the Gulf of Finland, or the 'ideal city' proposed for the Oktyabrskaya Embankment in St Petersburg, the geometry prevails; in the projects that are interventions in the existing urban fabric, the geometry recedes into the background. The competition entry for the revitalization of the New Holland area of St Petersburg, and the competition-winning idea for the Konyeshennaya and North Kolomna districts in the old part of Leningrad, are testaments to the studio's belief in careful integration.

A balancing act between integration and reinvention is at the heart of the studio's competition-winning proposal for the redevelopment of the historic centre of Kaliningrad (formerly known as Königsberg), which, after being almost completely destroyed during the Second World War, was rebuilt according to the then prevailing ideology of replacing the ruins of the past with new architecture and planning. Studio 44 proposes to bring back the structure, scale and character of pre-war Königsberg, without reverting to literal architectural reconstruction.

Hans Ibelings

27

HIGH-RISE BUILDINGS NEAR LADOZHSKY RAILWAY STATION

The square next to Ladozhsky railway station (see page 85) is an important town-planning and transport hub with a high concentration of activity generated by people and businesses. The area requires planning and development in order to realize its value and potential in the structure of the city. At such locations, high-rise buildings are a natural option; and not just one skyscraper, but a whole cluster of these imposing structures.

Five towers placed in the corners of a perfect pentagon reinforce the sense of an important urban hub within the larger city. This effect, however, is kept strictly local: approximately 150 metres high, the towers cannot be seen from the historical centre of St Petersburg, but will be visible from Alexander Nevsky Bridge. The buildings are all the same height in order to create a sense of regularity and unity.

Each tower is composed of two intersecting volumes. Owing to the configuration of the site, the ground-floor plans of the buildings have irregular forms; the flat roofs, by contrast, are regularly shaped. The design of each tower reflects the demand for office space in such buildings. The highest demand is for space on the lower floors, after which rental interest gradually falls; then, after reaching a minimum somewhere around the middle to two-thirds up, it rises again towards the top.

Square next to Ladozhsky railway station at the intersection of Zanevsky Prospekt and Prospekt Energetikov, St Petersburg, Russia

CLIENT: Adamant Kapital
DESIGN: 2006–7
REALIZATION: N/A
TOTAL AREA: 69,047 sq m (building no. 1)

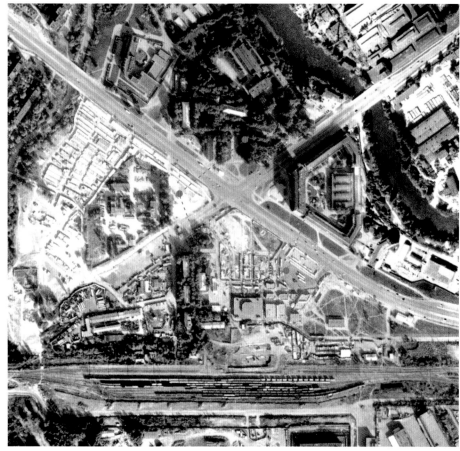

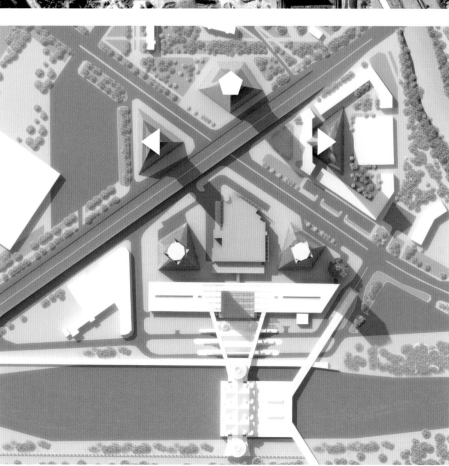

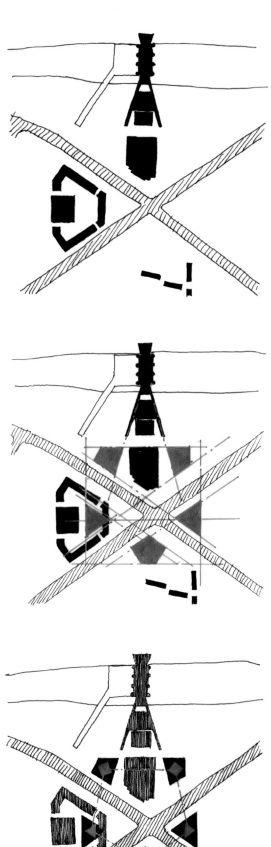

OPPOSITE, TOP LEFT
Topology of the design solution.

OPPOSITE, BOTTOM LEFT
General plan.

OPPOSITE, RIGHT
Diagram showing how the location
of existing buildings determined the
design of the new towers.

RIGHT
The construction volumes of
each tower.

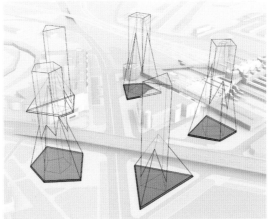

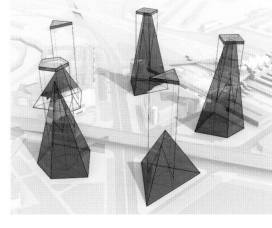

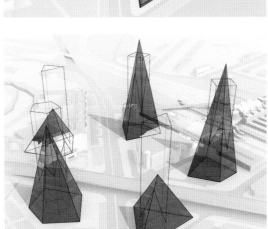

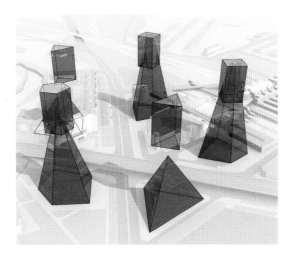

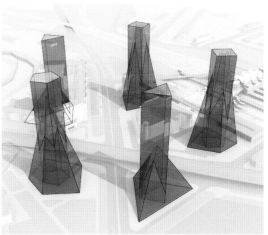

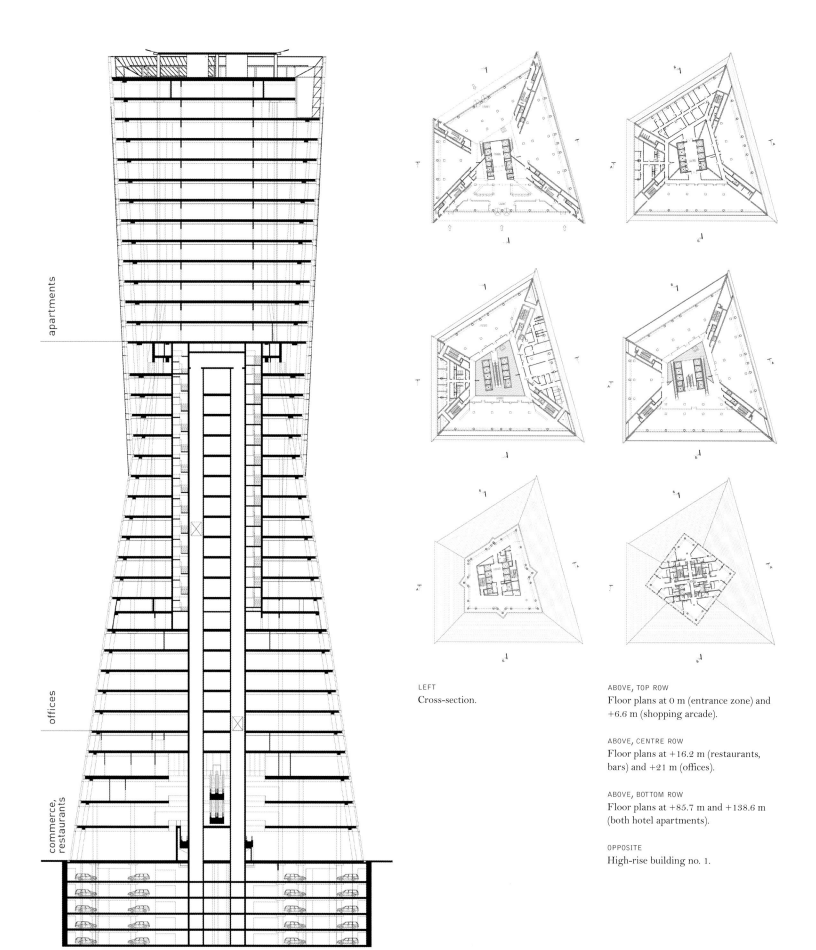

apartments

offices

commerce, restaurants

LEFT
Cross-section.

ABOVE, TOP ROW
Floor plans at 0 m (entrance zone) and +6.6 m (shopping arcade).

ABOVE, CENTRE ROW
Floor plans at +16.2 m (restaurants, bars) and +21 m (offices).

ABOVE, BOTTOM ROW
Floor plans at +85.7 m and +138.6 m (both hotel apartments).

OPPOSITE
High-rise building no. 1.

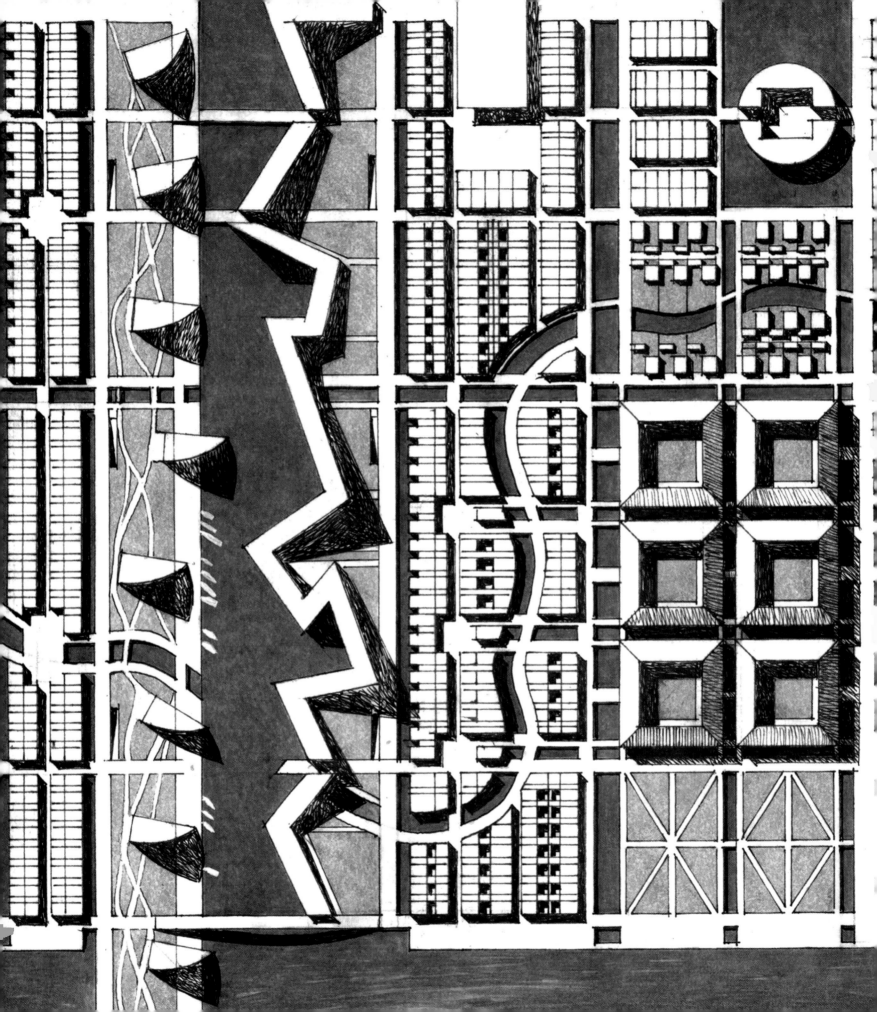

28

CITY ON THE WATER: RESIDENTIAL DISTRICT IN COASTAL AREA

This project revives the original idea of St Petersburg as a city on the water, with a regularized canal network throughout. Its spatial conception is based on the union and conflict between densely developed neighbourhoods and open expanses of water. The project is laid out in such a way that, like in Venice, each building can be accessed by boat; unlike in Venice, however, each building can also be reached by car.

The proposal is to fill a newly created system of islands and peninsulas with different types of buildings for both permanent and temporary residence. Various combinations of interconnected two- and three-storey houses form the urban fabric of the district. The range of houses also includes a higher class of property: individual villas with gardens, and estates on private islands.

Against this basic network, town planning takes place at a larger scale: residential buildings of different configurations and with varying numbers of storeys, twenty-five-storey tower blocks, and so on. Such buildings form key focal points and act as spatial coordinates for the entire district.

The district's infrastructure is centred on the mainland, with schools, nurseries and multipurpose complexes combining, among other things, various shopping, entertainment, service and medical facilities.

The Gulf of Finland near St Petersburg, Russia

CLIENT: Private individual
DESIGN: 2008
REALIZATION: N/A
TOTAL AREA: 1,456,000 sq m

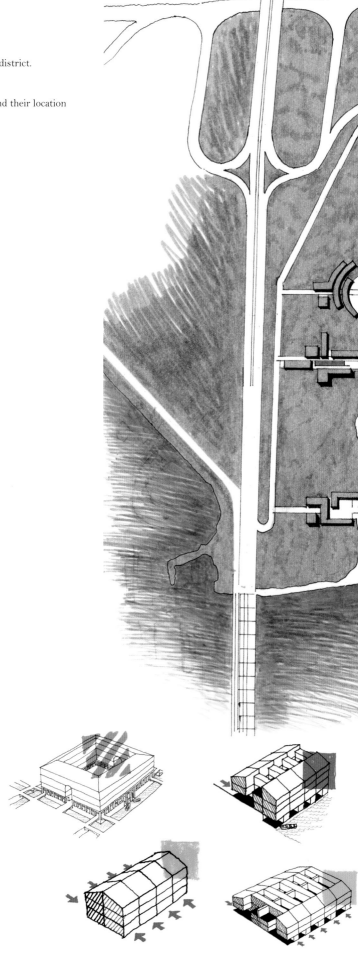

RIGHT
General plan of the district.

RIGHT, BOTTOM
Types of building and their location
in the district.

ABOVE
Master plan for St Petersburg by
architect Jean-Baptiste Le Blond, 1717.

BELOW
Detail of the master plan for
St Petersburg by architect Domenico
Trezzini, 1716.

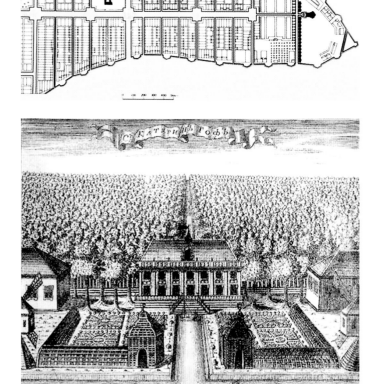

ABOVE
Ekaterinhof during the time of Peter
the Great. Engraving by Aleksey
Zubov, 1716.

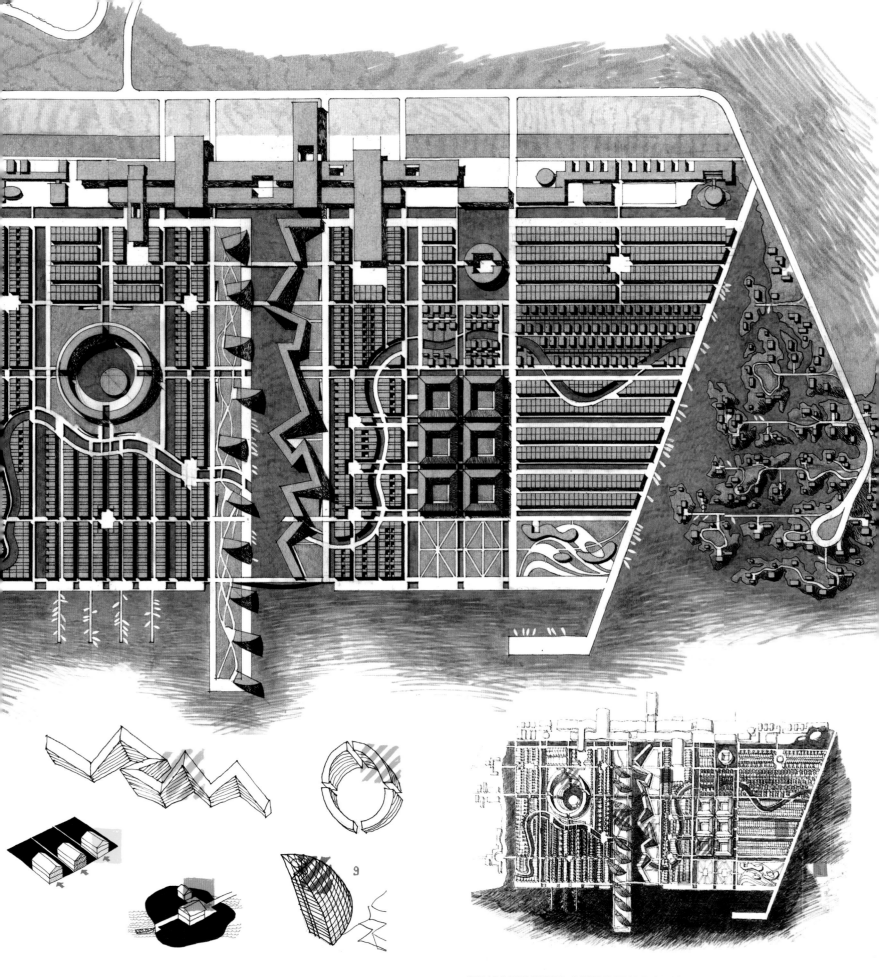

29

RESIDENTIAL QUARTER ON OKTYABRSKAYA EMBANKMENT

A residential quarter for 12,000 people, with almost half a million square metres of floor space, is equivalent to a small European city. With this in mind, the quarter proposed for Oktyabrskaya Embankment is conceived as an 'ideal city', arranged in a classical orthogonal grid composed of blocks measuring 100 × 100 m (for comparison, a residential quarter in the centre of Barcelona has 113 × 113-m blocks). This 'ideal city' contains all the elements one would expect to find in a traditional urban environment: the city wall and gate, the town square, the park, the street, the boulevard, and so on.

The compositional nucleus of the residential quarter is a landscaped square measuring 90 × 90 m, conceived as the quarter's main public space. The uniform, geometric grid plan guarantees logical movement and easy navigation: the north–south roads are for vehicles, while the pedestrian boulevards running east–west lead to the Neva River.

The residential buildings are arranged in square formations. There are two types of such building – one for small families and one for large – laid out in a chessboard-like arrangement. Along the southern edge of the quarter, nine residential buildings are stretched out in a line, forming a type of city wall. The southern entrance to the quarter is flanked by two 70-m towers containing studio apartments.

An essential part of the residential quarter's architectural landscape are the 'keepsakes of history': the red-brick buildings of the Vargunin paper factory and Thornton wool mill, restored and adapted to serve a variety of modern purposes.

54 Oktyabrskaya Embankment, St Petersburg, Russia

CLIENT: BFA Development
DESIGN: 2013 (1st place in competition)
REALIZATION: N/A
TOTAL AREA: 470,600 sq m

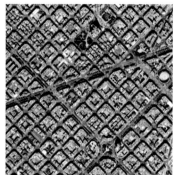

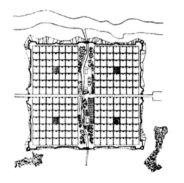

CLOCKWISE FROM FAR LEFT
Prototypes of an ideal city: central Creon, France; detail of a residential quarter in central Barcelona; master plan for St Petersburg (Jean-Baptiste Le Blond, 1717); plan of Amaurot, an ideal city (Thomas Moore, 1512).

ABOVE, LEFT AND RIGHT
Existing industrial buildings on Oktyabrskaya Embankment in 2014.

BELOW
Formulation of the architectural/planning solutions for the quarter.

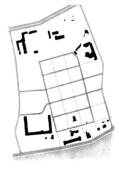

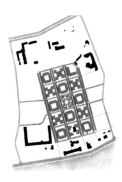

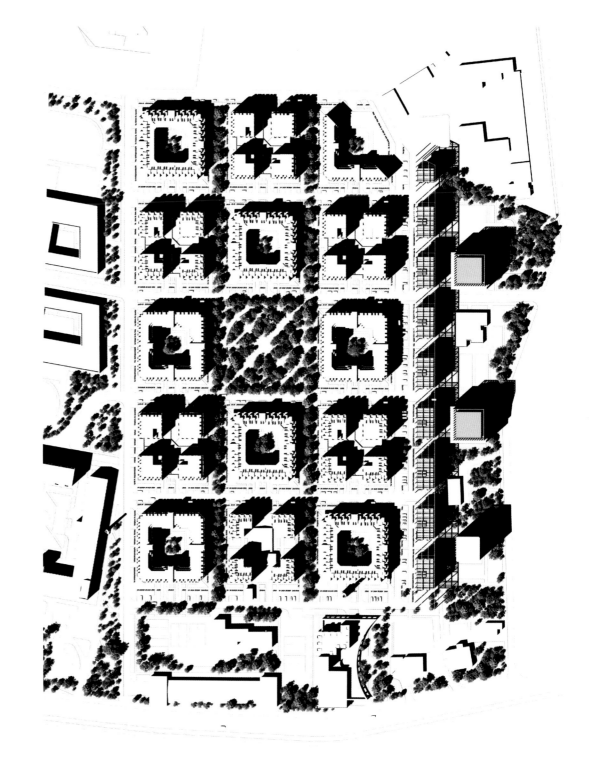

BELOW
Location of the various building types
(in red, from left): residential blocks
for large families; residential blocks
for small families; detached residential
blocks; tower blocks; school; hotel
complex.

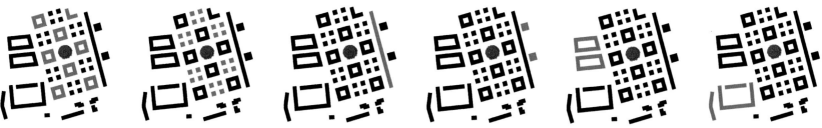

LEFT
Façades, cross-sections and plans of the large-family and small-family residential blocks.

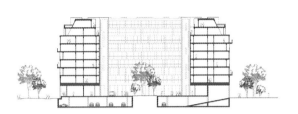

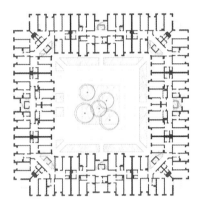

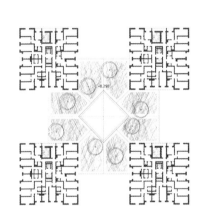

LEFT
Sketch of the central square, the quarter's main public space.

30

CENTRE OF MODERN CULTURE AT NEW HOLLAND

Revitalization of an 18th-century industrial complex

New Holland is a unique monument to early classical industrial architecture, located on a triangular, man-made island. The New Holland regeneration project will transform it into a multipurpose complex accommodating contemporary art, design and fashion exhibitions, as well as film, experimental theatre and music festivals.

New Holland's historical buildings comprise fifty large storage units, each measuring $33 \times 9 \times 20$ m, which were used to dry timber for shipbuilding. While completely preserving the buildings' authentic architecture, the regeneration project provides examples of how these units can be adapted to a wide range of uses, from exhibition halls to auditoriums to lofts.

The inner part of the complex has a small lake at its centre, and is conceived as an informal public area for socializing and leisure activities. This is a place where people can come to sunbathe and swim in the summer and ice-skate in the winter; where installations can be displayed and outdoor cinema screenings and rock concerts held. A system of locks, without hampering small boats, makes it possible to clean, heat and freeze the lake, as well as dry it out for use as a stage.

One of the buildings planned for the perimeter of the original complex was never constructed. It is proposed that a 'ship grove' be planted at this spot, in reference to the mast timber that used to be stored here. In this way, the outline of the complex makes a full circle, but one that is still see-through. While new bridges improve the island's links with the mainland, it still retains the romantic aura of an impregnable fortress.

2 Admiralteyskovo Kanala Embankment, St Petersburg, Russia

CLIENT: The Iris Foundation, New Holland Development
DESIGN: 2011 (international competition design)
REALIZATION: N/A
TOTAL AREA: 7.8 ha

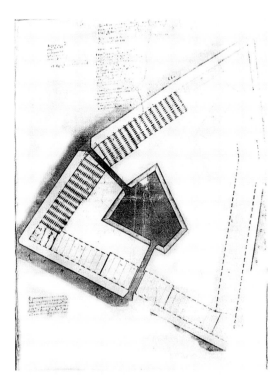

THIS PAGE
Design drawings from 1765 of the
iconographic New Holland warehouses.

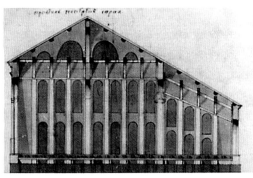

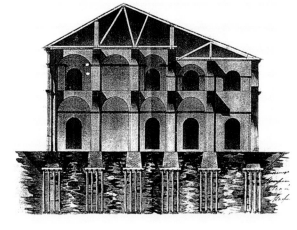

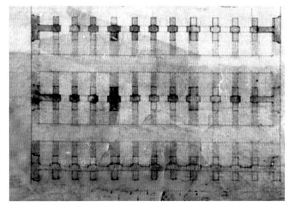

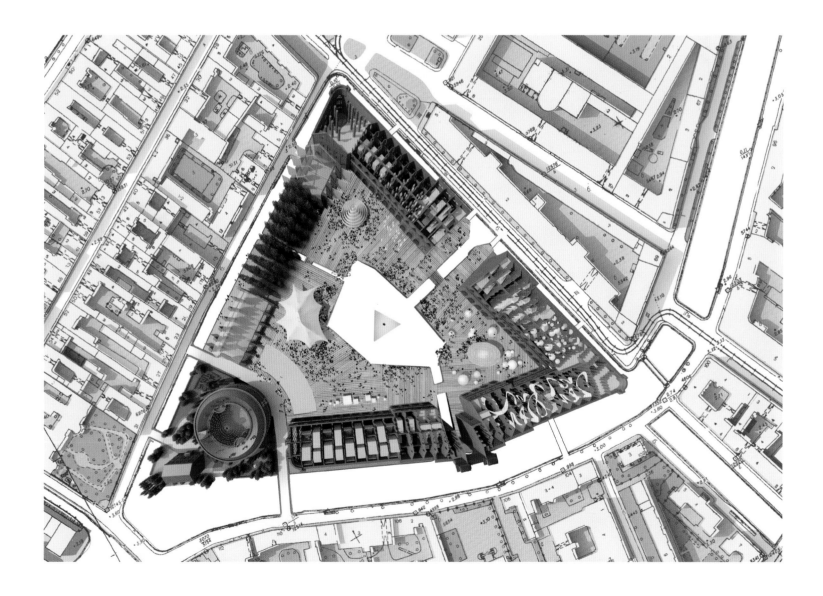

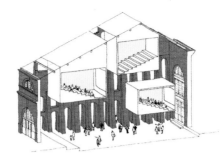

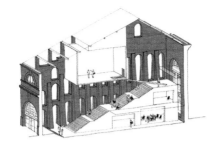

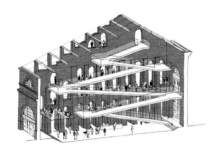

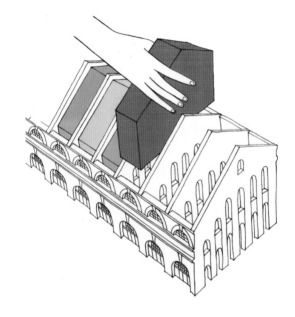

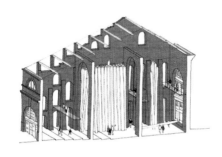

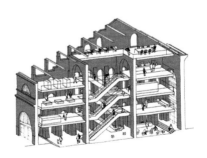

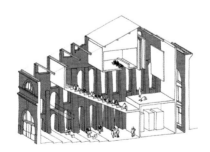

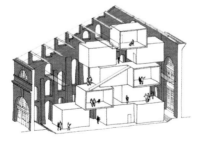

The former timber-drying units can
assume a wide range of functions.
Examples include (clockwise from top
left) a cinema, an auditorium, an event
space, a museum, exhibition spaces,
a theatre, retail and lofts.

OPPOSITE, TOP
Model of New Holland.

OPPOSITE, BOTTOM LEFT
Sketch of the internal volumes of
the former timber-drying units.

OPPOSITE, BOTTOM RIGHT
The 'ship grove', a green area filling
an undeveloped area of the complex.

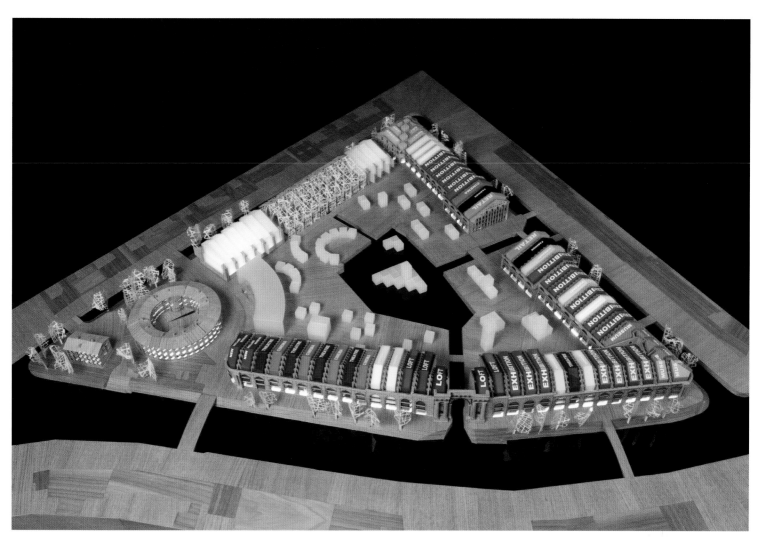

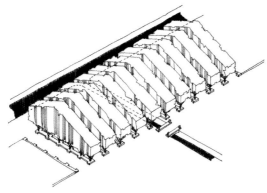

OVERLEAF
New Holland will receive several more bridges, but this will not detract from the sense of being on an unassailable fortress.

LEFT
The inner part of New Holland and Palace Square are characteristically different, yet serve to complement each other.

BELOW
Left to right, from top left: the inner area of the complex in winter, spring, summer and autumn.

RIGHT
The entrance loggia marks the
border between the inner area and
the cultural centre.

BELOW
The inner part of New Holland as
an open-air concert space.

A single exhibition space within the former timber-drying units.

31

DEVELOPMENT CONCEPT FOR KONYUSHENNAYA AND NORTH KOLOMNA NEIGHBOURHOODS IN HISTORICAL CENTRE OF ST PETERSBURG

One distinctive feature of St Petersburg, in comparison with other European cities, is its sparse network of streets and the sheer size of its residential blocks. This often leads to deterioration in the centre of the blocks, providing, in turn, a dramatic contrast to their luxurious façades.

The authors of the development concept regard the creation of a system of public spaces as a powerful incentive for the revitalization of the city. Branching off from the main pedestrian arteries, the public spaces flow naturally into the neighbourhoods, forming a network of 'capillaries'. This gives the effect of breaking up the neighbourhoods: their accessible perimeter is increased, creating the conditions needed to stimulate business activity, balance property prices, revitalize dilapidated zones and improve the quality of the area and living conditions.

Delving deep into the St Petersburg that is hidden from view, the authors of the concept compiled an inventory of neglected spaces that could be transformed into pedestrianized streets, small squares and even parks. These new public spaces have been brought together in a systemic way, and means to link them to the main tourist attractions of the central districts have been developed. The traffic network is filled with bicycle lanes and lanes for alternative transportation.

The concept offers a financial model for the area's transformation, in which city funds go towards the implementation of the infrastructural part of the programme, thus bringing private investment into the improvement of old residential buildings.

St Petersburg, Russia

CLIENT: The Government of St Petersburg
DESIGN: 2012 (1st place in competition)
REALIZATION: N/A
TOTAL AREA: 124 ha

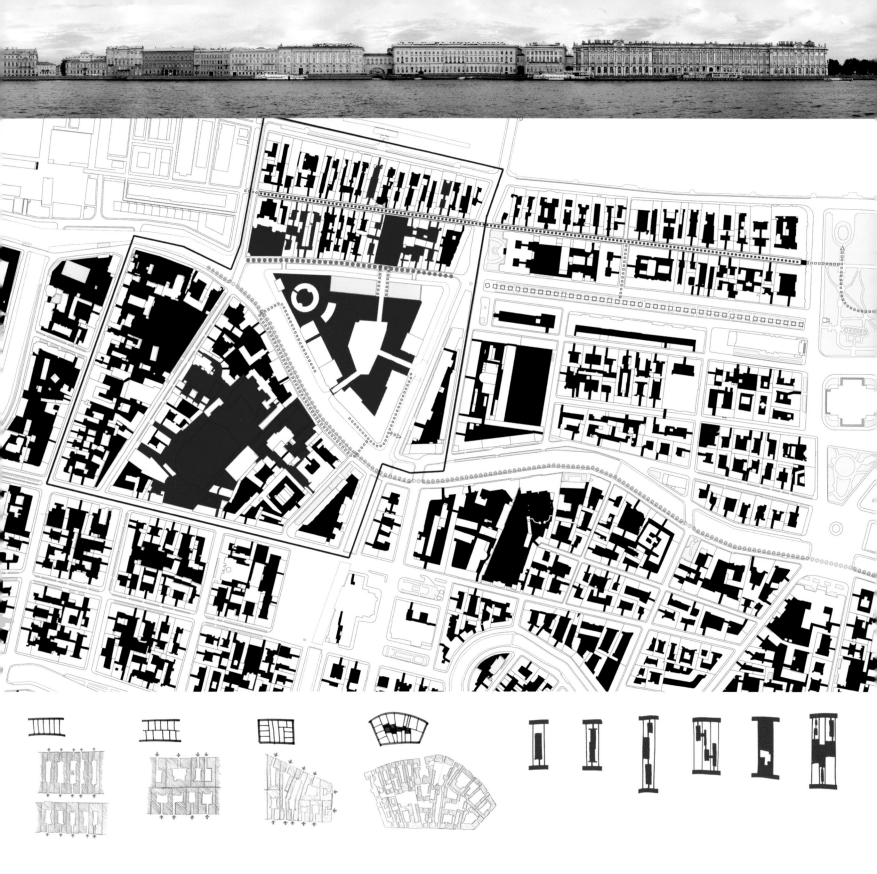

ABOVE, TOP
Panorama of the Palace Embankment.

ABOVE, CENTRE
General plan.

ABOVE, LEFT
Building morphotypes for
central residential developments
in St Petersburg.

ABOVE
Type of urban-fabric border system:
'street–courtyard–street'.

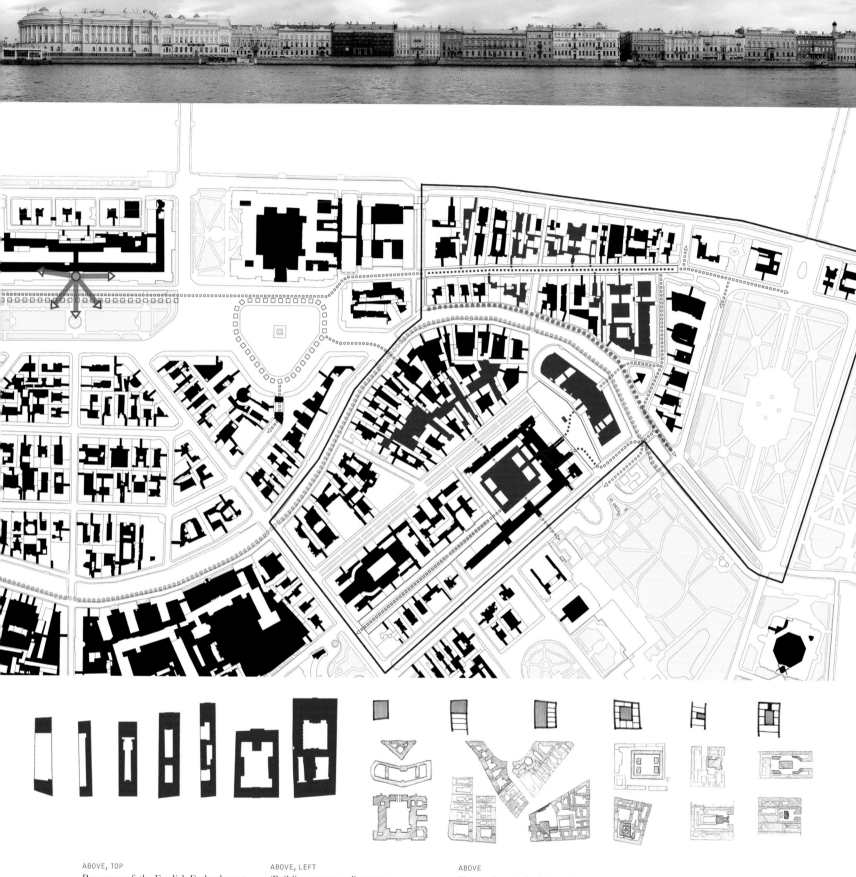

ABOVE, TOP
Panorama of the English Embankment.

ABOVE, LEFT
'Building–courtyard' system
building modules.

ABOVE
Types of mutual relationship in
a 'facility–urban fabric' system.

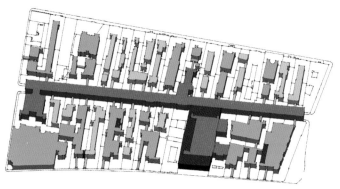

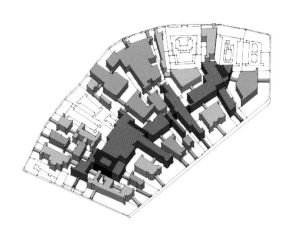

■ Buildings earmarked for demolition

■ Public space

■ Areas earmarked for inclusion in public space

▨ Other possible public spaces

STUDIO 44

OPPOSITE, FROM TOP
System of public spaces along
Millionnaya Street (from Field of
Mars to the Winter Canal); in the
area around Dekabrist Street; along
Galernaya Street (from Labour Square
to New Holland Island); and in the
Chapel Courtyards area.

THIS PAGE
Conceptual sketches of the public
spaces.

32

CONCEPT FOR THE DEVELOPMENT OF THE HISTORICAL CENTRE OF KALININGRAD

Studio 44's concept is a response to the nostalgia the citizens of Kaliningrad feel for the old town of Königsberg – the town that was razed to the ground in 1944-6, the town they know only from photographs. It is accepted that Königsberg was built to a more human scale; that it was more diverse and more spectacular than the post-war Kaliningrad that was built on top of its ruins. The development concept is an attempt to restore the historic town as an example of urban and environmental planning.

The old Königsberg was comprised of parts with very different characters (Altstadt, Lastadie, Vorstadt, Lomse, etc.). Studio 44's concept is aimed at restoring the diversity of yesteryear, not by reproducing original buildings, but by reproducing structure, scale and character. For this purpose, local regulations were written, laying down the requirements concerning dimensions of buildings, roof and window configurations, finishing materials, etc.

The strictest regulations apply to Altstadt, where, buried under a two-metre layer of soil, the foundations and cellars of ancient buildings can be found.

In Altstadt, archaeological excavations would be undertaken, with surviving basements cleaned and restored. The surviving building foundations would be reinforced. In areas between buildings, soil would be removed down to the level of the deepest basement. At this level, new small town squares would be established.

The new Königsberg would grow out of the ruins of the old, with the walls of new buildings acting as extensions of the surviving ground-floor walls. The new central districts would provide an environment for the return of traditional ways of life, with small manufacturing firms and shops at ground-floor level, apartments on the upper floors, and pedestrian-friendly narrow streets and small squares.

Kaliningrad, Russia

CLIENT: The Government of Kaliningrad Region
DESIGN: 2014 (1st place in international competition)
REALIZATION: N/A
TOTAL AREA: 70 ha

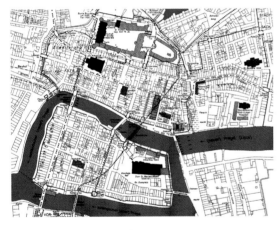

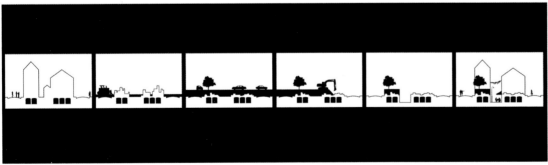

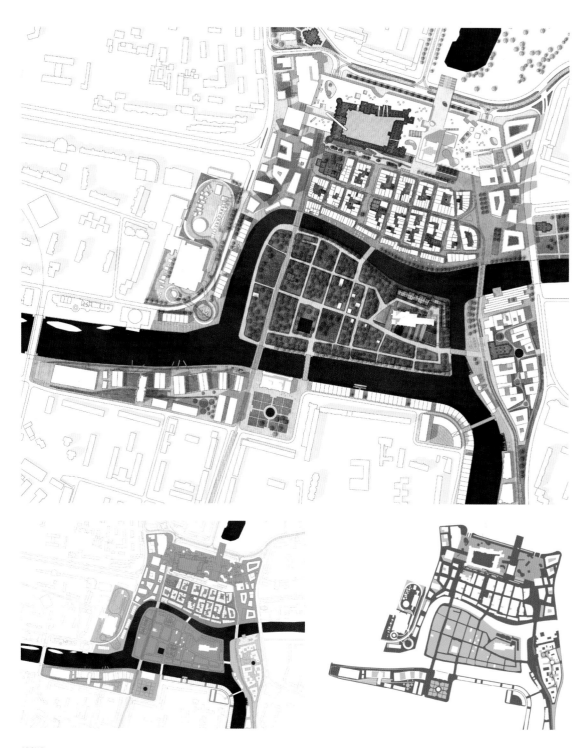

ABOVE
Map showing the different zones
of development.

ABOVE, RIGHT
Scheme of pedestrianized zones
and green spaces.

Archive photograph of Altstadt.

Altstadt building regulations..

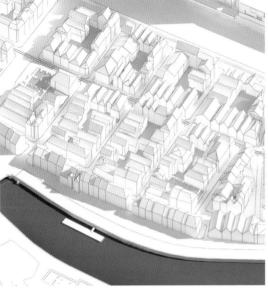

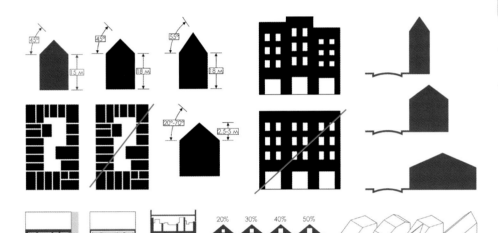

ABOVE
Proposal for the development
of Altstadt.

BELOW, CLOCKWISE FROM TOP LEFT
Urban environment of new Altstadt;
public space by the former Soviet
House; archaeological excavation phase
of regeneration of Altstadt.

ABOVE
Historical and contemporary brickwork
in the redevelopment of Altstadt.

LEFT
Proposal for the redevelopment
of Lastadie.

20%   30%   40%   50%

55°

18 M

LEFT
Lastadie building regulations.

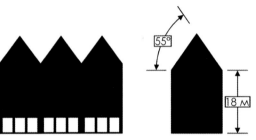

LEFT
General view of the proposed
redevelopment of Lastadie.

RIGHT
Archive photo of Kneiphof Island.

CENTRE AND FAR RIGHT
Breakdown of the park on Kneiphof Island.

BELOW
View of the cathedral on Kneiphof Island

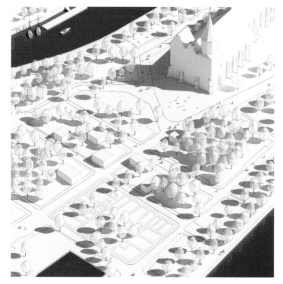

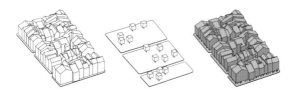

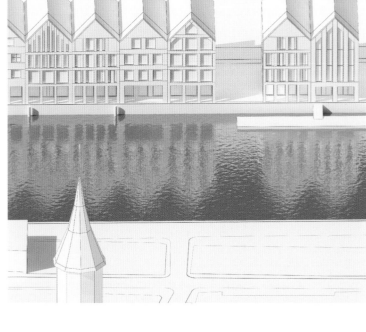

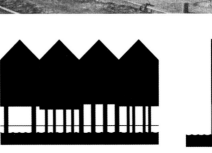

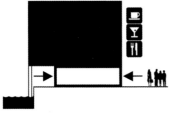

ABOVE, TOP
Archive photo of Eastern Vorstadt.

ABOVE, TOP RIGHT
Proposal for the redevelopment of
Eastern Vorstadt.

ABOVE
Building regulations for Eastern
Vorstadt.

RIGHT
General view of the proposed
redevelopment of Eastern Vorstadt.

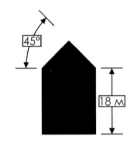

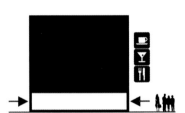

ABOVE, TOP
Archive photo of West Vorstadt.

ABOVE, TOP RIGHT
Proposal for the redevelopment of
West Vorstadt.

ABOVE
Building regulations for West Vorstadt.

RIGHT
General view of the proposed
redevelopment of West Vorstadt.

View of Altstadt from the
observation platform.

ABOUT STUDIO 44

Studio 44 Architects is one of the largest private architectural firms not only in St Petersburg but also in Russia. The studio's team consists of about 150 highly qualified specialists in a variety of fields (architects, restoration experts, structural designers, engineers). Twenty-five specialists are currently running and coordinating ongoing projects and acting as chief architects, chief structural designers and chief engineers.

At the company's core are specialists with ten to fifteen years' experience, and this staff base is constantly being added to through the addition of talented young professionals.

Studio 44 performs the whole cycle of design research – from concepts and preliminary sketches to working drawings – and prepares the complete set of design documentation. The company has extensive experience in acting as general designer and coordinating contractor work. The firm provides a range of services, including technical support during approval procedures and help with state inspection of design documentation, as well as architectural supervision of the construction process.

The company specializes in designing large public venues and multipurpose complexes: cultural and educational centres; trade, office and bank buildings; museums; theatres; stations; and medical and sporting facilities. Studio 44's portfolio includes domestic housing projects not only for individual homes but also for entire neighbourhood apartment developments. In its planning and conceptual research, Studio 44 focuses on the quality of living, the creation of shared public spaces, accessibility to transport and pedestrian access.

Studio 44 boasts unique experience in the reconstruction of old buildings, the restoration and adaptation of cultural heritage buildings, and the revitalization of large fragments of historic housing developments. Within the sphere of restoration work, Studio 44 markets itself as a company capable of transforming the existing city fabric, each time striking an optimum balance between old and new, tradition and modernity.

The strong professional reputation of Studio 44 is reinforced by more than ninety prestigious awards garnered by the company for building and renovation projects, including the Russian Federation (RF) State Prize (1998) and the RF Government Prize for Culture (2015), as well as a host of significant national architectural accolades, such as the Crystal Daedalus (2001, 2004, 2012), the Vladimir Tatlin Prize (2011, 2014) and the Sergey Kiselev 'Reputation' Prize (2015). Studio 44 is a frequent participant in and winner of the St Petersburg Arkitekton show and competition, and the international Architecture festival in Moscow; it is also a regular exhibitor at the architectural biennales in Moscow and St Petersburg. Studio 44 has twice presented Russian architecture in Venice (2008, 2010). In 2015, Studio 44 was awarded the main prizes at the World Architecture Festival (WAF) in two categories: 'Completed Buildings: Schools' and 'Future Projects: Masterplanning'.

MANAGEMENT AND STRUCTURE

MANAGEMENT
Head: Nikita Yawein
Director: Lyudmila Vygovskaya
Deputy Director: Alexander Kosharny
Research: Oleg Yawein
PR and communication: Lyudmila Likhacheva

STRUCTURE
The firm consists of four main departments:

Architectural Studio 1
Head: Nikita Yawein
Specialist area: transport venues, new construction and reconstruction in city centres, competition and concept design

Architectural Studio 2
Head: Grigory Ivanov
Specialist area: reconstruction of historic buildings, restoration of cultural heritage monuments and their adaptation for contemporary uses

Architectural Studio 3
Head: Nikolay Smolin
Specialist area: large, technologically complex public venues (cultural, medical, educational, sports, recreational and retail)

Structural Design Department
Head: Dmitry Kresov
Specialist area: development of structural solutions for all the studio's projects

NIKITA YAWEIN

Nikita Yawein is recognized as one of Russia's leading architects, and informally considered one of the country's foremost leaders by the Russian architectural community. His concepts, designs and projects have had a significant influence on the development of architectural thought in Russia.

Yawein, the founder and head of Studio 44 Architects, quickly gained recognition after graduating from college, owing in large part to a series of highly original design-competition entries. For about ten years he chaired the St Petersburg Committee for the Conservation of Architectural and Cultural Monuments. Yawein is the originator of more than 150 projects in various cities and regions of Russia and abroad, a third of which have been implemented. The designs and developments of Yawein and his colleagues differ constantly in terms of strategy and style, depending on the historical context and location of the project.

CURRICULUM VITAE

1954 Born in Leningrad into the family of architect Igor Georgievich Yawein

1977 Completed studies at the Leningrad Institute of Engineering and Construction, architectural faculty

1977–92 Worked in state design institutions

1992 Founded his own architectural bureau

1994–2003 Committee representative for government control, use and conservation of St Petersburg monuments

2003–present Head of Studio 44 Architects

Laureate of the RF State Prize for Literature and Art (1998)
Laureate of the RF Government Prize for Culture (2015)
Winner of the Crystal Daedalus (2001, 2004, 2012) and the Vladimir Tatlin Prize (2011, 2014)
Active member of the Russian Academy for Architecture and Civil Engineering
Member of the St Petersburg Town Planning Council
Member of the council for the preservation of the cultural heritage of St Petersburg
Professor at St Petersburg Art Academy

LIST OF COMPLETED PROJECTS

2016 Kazakh National Academy of Choreography, Astana, Kazakhstan

2015 Campus of Graduate School of Management, St Petersburg University, Russia

2014 State Hermitage Museum in the East Wing of the General Staff Building, St Petersburg, Russia

2014 Treatment/rehabilitation complex at the V.A. Almazov Federal Centre for Heart, Blood and Endocrinology, St Petersburg, Russia

2013 Olympic Park railway station, Sochi, Russia

2012 Boris Eifman Dance Academy, St Petersburg, Russia

2011 Palace of Schoolchildren, Astana, Kazakhstan

2010 New Peterhof Hotel, St Petersburg, Russia

2009 Studio 44 offices, St Petersburg, Russia

2009 Linkor Business Centre, St Petersburg, Russia

2009 Office building on Telezhnaya Street, St Petersburg, Russia

2006 Residential building on 10th Sovietskaya Street, St Petersburg, Russia

2004 Nevsky 38 Business Centre, St Petersburg, Russia

2004 Residential building at Krestyansky Lane, St Petersburg, Russia

2004 Residential building at 43 Kirochnaya Street, St Petersburg, Russia

2003 Ladozhsky railway station, St Petersburg, Russia

2003 Grand Palace shopping arcade, St Petersburg, Russia

2003 Pur Navolok Hotel, Archangelsk, Russia

2003 Residential building at 24 Konnaya Street, St Petersburg, Russia

2002 Pavilion in the MGU botanical garden, Moscow, Russia

2001 Residential building at 7 Sofiysky Boulevard, Pushkin, St Petersburg, Russia

2001 Restoration of the railway station, Veliky Novgorod, Russia

1998 Operational management, Sberbank, St Petersburg, Russia

1998 Administration department, Sberbank, St Petersburg, Russia

1998 Vasileyostrovsky branch, Sberbank, St Petersburg, Russia

1997 Atrium at Nevsky 25 Business Centre, St Petersburg, Russia

1996 Country house for Yawein family, Leningrad Region, Russia

1990 Kremlin Housing Community, Solovetsky, Bolshoi Solovetsky Island, Arkhangelsk Region, Russia

PROJECT CREDITS

1. The Cube Residential Estate
Architect: Nikita Yawein

2. A Home for Three Generations of One Family
Architect: Nikita Yawein
With contributions from Oleg Yawein

3. Signal Children's Pioneer Camp
Architect: Nikita Yawein
Structural engineer: Leonid Kaplan

4. Amphitheatre of Boxes
Architects: Igor Yawein, Nikita Yawein, Oleg Yawein

5. Kremlin Housing Community
Architects: Nikita Yawein, Svetlana Borisenkova, Vitaly Antipin,
    with contributions from Olga Igonina, Margarita Yawein
Structural engineer: Leonid Kaplan
General contractor: Capital Construction Administration of
    the Arkhangelsk Regional Executive Committee

6. Nursery School Building, Kremlin Housing Community
Architects: Nikita Yawein, Svetlana Borisenkova, with
    contributions from Vitaly Antipin, Margarita Yawein
Structural engineer: Leonid Kaplan

7. Solovki Airport Hotel
Architects: Nikita Yawein, Nina Balazh

8. Yaweins' Country House
Architects: Nikita Yawein, Oleg Yawein, with contributions
    from Margarita Yawein

9. Central Branch of Sberbank of Russia, St Petersburg
Reconstruction of properties from the second half of the
    nineteenth century
Architects: Nikita Yawein, Nina Balazh, with contributions
    from Vladimir Zenkevich, Vladimir Parfyonov
Structural engineer: Veniamin Kuper
General contractor: OJSC 'GRST-1' (The Municipal Building
    and Repairs Trust)

10. Ladozhsky Railway Station
Architects: Nikita Yawein, Vladimir Zenkevich, Vasily Romantsev,
    Zhanna Razumova, with contributions from Elena Barykina,
    Irina Golysheva, Grigory Ivanov, Irina Krylova, Lyudmila
    Kutuzova, Andrey Medvedev, Sergey Sologub, Elizaveta Fokina
Structural engineers: Yury Bondarev, Irina Lyashko,
    Irina Gracheva, N.V. Kozlov, Ekaterina Khlybova
General contractor: Baltic Construction Company

11. Residential Building, Krestyansky Lane
Architects: Nikita Yawein, Vladimir Parfyonov,
    with contributions from Ekaterina Kobozeva
Structural engineers: Yury Bondarev, Irina Lyashko
General contractor: CJSC BSK PGS

12. Nevsky 38 Business Centre
Reconstruction and restoration of architectural monuments
    from the first third of the eighteenth century
Architects: Nikita Yawein, Vitaly Antipin, Valery Kulachenkov,
    Pavel Sokolov, with contributions from Pyotr Berezin,
    Vladimir Zenkevich, Maryam Zamelova, Lyudmila
    Kutuzova, Vladimir Parfyonov, Natalia Pobedinskaya,
    Zhanna Razumova, Tatiana Sologub, Varvara Khmelyova
Restorers: Mikhailov Architectural Studio
Structural engineers: Oleg Kurbatov, Boris Mironkov
General contractor: OJSC 'TsentrInvestStroi'

13. Residential Building, 10th Sovietskaya Street
Architects: Nikita Yawein, Vladimir Parfyonov, Zhanna
    Razumova, with contributions from Elena Barykina, Grigory
    Ivanov, Ekaterina Kobozeva, Anastasia Skorik, Lyubov Usova
Structural engineers: Yury Bondarev, Irina Lyashko, Irina
    Gracheva, Irina Nikulina
General contractor: OJSC 'GRST-1'

14. Studio 44 Offices
Reconstruction of a building from the beginning of the
    twentieth century
Architects: Nikita Yawein, Vasily Romantsev, Tatiana Sologub,
    Georgy Snezhkin, Ksenia Schastlivtseva
Structural engineer: Dmitry Yaroshevsky
General contractor: OJSC 'Gradstroi'
Construction of wood frame structure: Okonnaya Verf design
    and construction company

15. Linkor Business Centre

Reconstruction of industrial buildings from the 1970s

Architects: Nikita Yawein, Valery Kulachenkov, Vladimir Lemekhov, Pavel Sokolov, with contributions from Tatiana Vasilyeva, Olga Volkova, Maryam Zamelova, Dmitry Kosov, Tatiana Sologub, Varvara Khmelyova

Structural engineers: Oleg Kurbatov, Vladimir Ioffe, Sergey Romantsev

16. New Peterhof Hotel

Architects: Nikita Yawein, Vladimir Zenkevich, Vitaly Antipin, Grigory Ivanov, with contributions from Elena Loginova, Yanina Reut, Anastasia Skorik, Pyotr Shlikhter

Structural engineers: Irina Lyashko, Irina Grachyova, Irina Nikulina, Natalia Prosvetova

ISU: Vladimir Kremlyovsky

General contractor: TNG Group (Serbia)

17. The State Hermitage Museum in the East Wing of the General Staff Building

Restoration of architectural monument from the first third of the nineteenth century and its adapation in line with new uses

Architects: Oleg Yawein, Nikita Yawein, Vladimir Lemekhov, Pavel Sokolov, with contributions from Vitaly Antipin, Irina Golysheva, Sergey Dryazzhin, Evgeny Elovkov, Veronika Zhukova, Irina Krylova, Vladimir Parfyonov, Georgy Snezhkin, Sergey Sologub, Varvara Khmelyova, Anton Yar-Skryabin

Restorers: Grigory Mikhailov (Mikhailov Architectural Studio); Oleg Kuzevanov, Natalia Shirokova (Studio 44 Architects)

Structural engineers: Vladimir Ioffe, Dmitry Kresov, Oleg Kurbatov, Irina Lyashko, Dmitry Yaroshevsky

Museum exhibition lighting: Cannon-Brookes Lighting & Design (Great Britain)

General contractor: OJSC 'Integration' Construction Company

18. Astana Railway Station

Architects: Nikita Yawein, Vladimir Zenkevich, Sergey Aksyonov, Yury Ashmetyev, Maria Vinogradova, Ilya Grigoryev, Veronika Zhukova, Ivan Kozhin, Vladimir Lemekhov, Evgeny Novosadyuk, Georgy Snezhkin, Anton Stanchinsky, Ksenia Schastlivtseva, Margarita Yawein

Structural engineer: Vladimir Gershtein

Mock-up: Yakov Itsikson

19. Palace of Schoolchildren

Winning project in international competition

Architects: Nikita Yawein, Sergey Aksyonov, Daria Gordina, Maryam Zamelova, Vladimir Zenkevich, Ivan Kozhin, Daria Nasonova, Natalia Poznyanskaya, Nikolay Smolin, Yanina Smolina, Georgy Snezhkin, with contributions from Natalia Arkhipova, Igor Britikov, Maria Vinogradova, Ilya Grigoryev, Nikita Zhukov, Veronika Zhukova, Evgenia Kuptsova, Elena Loginova, Nikolay Novotochinov, Ksenia Schastlivtseva, Anton Yar-Skryabin

Design-phase project documentation and working documentation developed in collaboration with specialists from Bazis-Projekt Ltd LLC (Almaty)

General contractor: Bazis A LLC construction company

20. Zhastar Youth Palace

Architects: Nikita Yawein, Maria Vinogradova, Daria Gordina, Vladimir Zenkevich, Ivan Kozhin, Vladimir Lemekhov, Vasily Romantsev, Anna Rudenko, Georgy Snezhkin, Ulyana Sulimova

Visualization: Andrey Patrikeyev

Head engineer: Lev Gershtein

Structural engineer: Yury Bondarev

Design-phase project documentation developed in collaboration with specialists from Bazis-Projekt Ltd:

Head architect: Elena Zenina

Head engineer: Nadezhda Dashko

Structural engineers: Mark Vainshtein, Gennady Sultanov

21. Football Stadium for 2018 FIFA World Cup

Architects: Nikita Yawein, Yury Ashmetyev, Daria Bazhenova, Maria Vinogradova, Ilya Grigoryev, Yulia Dubeiko, Vladimir Zenkevich, Ivan Kozhin, Vladimir Lemekhov, Evgeny Novosadyuk, Georgy Snezhkin, Ksenia Schastlivtseva, Anton Yar-Skryabin

Design: Yakov Itsikson

22. Olympic Park Railway Station

Architects: Nikita Yawein, Vladimir Zenkevich, Vasily Romantsev, Zhanna Razumova, Pyotr Shlikhter, with contributions from Maria Vinogradova, Veronika Zhukova, Irina Kalinyakova, Evgenia Kuptsova, Ulyana Sulimova, Ksenia Schastlivtseva

Structural engineers: Vladimir Gershtein, Dmitry Kresov, Rustem Akhimbekov, Andrey Krivonosov, Irina Lyashko, Natalia Prosvetova, Vladimir Turchevsky, Sergey Shvedov

(Studio 44 Architects); Yury Bondarev, Dmitry Nikitin (Tekton JSC)
ISU: Lev Gershtein, Vladimir Kremlyovsky
General contractor: Mostovik NGO

23. Tsar's Garden Hotel Complex
Architects: Nikita Yawein, Elizaveta Brilliantova, Dmitry Kozhin, Vladimir Lemekhov, Anna Rudenko, Anton Yar-Skryabin
Visualization: Andrey Patrikeyev, Vladimir Sokolov

24. Science and Technology Museum
Architects: Nikita Yawein, Anton Yar-Skryabin, with contributions from Alyona Amelkovich, Ivan Kozhin, Anna Kutilina, Roman Pokrovsky, Ksenia Schastlivtseva
Visualization: Aleksey Vetkin, Andrey Patrikeyev

25. Campus of Graduate School of Management, St Petersburg University
Architects: Nikita Yawein, Pavel Sokolov, Vasily Romantsev, Zhanna Razumova, Vladimir Parfyonov, with contributions from Tatiana Andreeva, Maria Vinogradova, Marina Goryachkina, Ilyana Donika, Evgeny Elovkov, Nikita Zhukov, Maryam Zamelova, Ekaterina Kobozeva, Lyudmila Kutuzova, Elena Loginova, Anastasia Skorik, Evgenia Sorokina, Pyotr Shlikhter
Restorers: Oleg Kuzevanov, Olga Rogacheva, Svetlana Morozova, Yulia Komarova, Grigory Mikhailov (JSC ASM), Larisa Odintsova (Lenproektrestavratsia)
Structural engineers: Irina Lyashko, Dmitry Kresov
General Contrator: JSC Settle City

26. Boris Eifman Dance Academy
Architects: Nikita Yawein, Sergey Aksyonov, Marina Goryachkina, Valery Kulachenkov, Georgy Snezhkin, with contributions from Aleksey Vetkin
Structural engineers: Vladimir Gershtein, Irina Lyashko, Dmitry Kresov, Natalia Prosvetova, Elena Silantyeva
General contractor: JSC TsentrInvestStroi

27. High-Rise Buildings near Ladozhsky Railway Station
Concept
Architects: Nikita Yawein, Natalia Arkhipova, Vladimir Zenkevich, Yury Ashmetyev

High-rise building no. 1
Architects: Nikita Yawein, Nikolay Smolin, Yanina Smolina, Daria Nasonova, with contributions from Igor Britikov, Evgeny Korepanov, Natalia Poznyanskaya
Structural engineers: Dmitry Kresov, Oleg Kurbatov, Irina Lyashko
Design: Yakov Itsikson

28. City on the Water: Residential District in Coastal Area
Architects: Nikita Yawein, Vladimir Lemekhov

29. Residential Quarter on Oktyabrskaya Embankment
Architects: Nikita Yawein, Yanina Smolina, Dmitry Kozhin, Ivan Kozhin, Vladimir Lemekhov, Evgeny Novosadyuk, Oksana Okladnikova, Andrey Patrikeyev, Anna Rudenko, Maria Sokolova, Aleksandra Fyodorova, Mikhail Fyodorov, Ekaterina Fedotova

30. Centre of Modern Culture at New Holland
Architects: Nikita Yawein, Sergey Aksyonov, Ilya Grigoryev, Ivan Kozhin, Vladimir Lemekhov, Georgy Snezhkin, Oleg Yawein, with contributions from Yury Ashmetyev, Maria Vinogradova, Veronika Zhukova, Ksenia Schastlivtseva, Anton Stanchinsky, Anton Yar-Skryabin
Design: Yakov Itsikson

31. Development Concept for Konyushennaya and North Kolomna Neighbourhoods
Architects: Nikita Yawein, Oleg Yawein, Maria Vinogradova, Ilya Grigoryev, Ivan Kozhin, Vladimir Lemekhov, Andrey Patrikeyev, Georgy Snezhkin

32. Concept for the Development of the Historical Centre of Kaliningrad
Architects: Nikita Yawein, Ilya Grigoryev, Ivan Kozhin, Ksenia Schastlivtseva
Visualization: Aleksey Vetkin, Andrey Patrikeyev
Project summary: Lyudmila Likhacheva
Traffic: Gennady Shelukhin (Territorial Development Institute)

PICTURE CREDITS

All photographs, illustrations, drawings and diagrams
© Studio 44 Architects unless otherwise indicated below.

9 (bottom): © Andrey Belimov-Guschin
10 (top): © Aleksey Naroditsky
11 (top): © Vadim Kekin
12 (top): © Maksim Atayants
13 (bottom): © Nikita and Oleg Yawein
15: © Vadim Yegorovsky
36 (right): © Nikita and Oleg Yawein
50: © Nikita and Oleg Yawein
52 (top left): © Igor Yawein
52 (top right): © Nikita and Oleg Yawein
52 (bottom right): © Nikita and Oleg Yawein
53 (both photographs): © Nikita and Oleg Yawein
54–5: © Nikita and Oleg Yawein
60 (centre left): © Yury Ushakov
70 (top): © Yury Gnatyuk
80 (top row, second from left): © Maksim Atayants
80 (top row, right): © Andrey Chernikhov
80 (bottom row, left): © Vadim Kekin
80 (bottom row, second from right): © Vadim Kekin
82: © Vadim Yegorovsky
84 (top): © Vadim Yegorovsky
84 (bottom left): © The Russian Art Academy Art & Science
    Museum
86 (all illustrations): © Vadim Yegorovsky
88 (top left and bottom left): © Vadim Yegorovsky
89: © Vadim Yegorovsky
90 (top left and bottom left): © Vadim Yegorovsky
91: © Vadim Yegorovsky
92: © Maksim Atayants
94 (top left): © Ivan Fomin
94 (left, second from bottom): © Igor Yawein
95: © Vadim Yegorovsky
98 (bottom left): © Vadim Yegorovsky
99: © Maksim Atayants
100 (top): © Maksim Atayants

100 (bottom): © Vadim Yegorovsky
102 (bottom left and bottom right): © Maksim Atayants
108: © Andrey Chernikhov
110 (right top and right centre): © State-run committee
    for the use and conservation of historical monuments
    and culture
113 (all photographs): © Andrey Chernikhov
114 (left): © Andrey Chernikhov
116 (all photographs except left): © Andrey Chernikhov
117: © Vadim Yegorovsky
118 (both photographs): © Vadim Yegorovsky
120: © Vadim Kekin
124 (top left and bottom left): © Vadim Kekin
129 (bottom): © Aleksey Naroditsky
130 (top left): © Georgy Snezhkin
130 (bottom left, top right and bottom right): © Aleksey
    Naroditsky
131 (top): © Aleksey Naroditsky
132: © Vadim Kekin
134 (bottom): © Vadim Kekin
136 (top left): © Yuri Molodkovets
136 (top right and bottom): © Vladimir Lemekhov
139 (all photographs): © Yury Molodkovets
144 (bottom left): © Vadim Kekin
146 (second row, second from left): © Aleksey Naroditsky
146 (bottom row, right): © Aleksey Naroditsky
159 (top left): © Anton Yar-Skryabin
172 (left): © Aleksey Naroditsky
173 (top): © Aleksey Naroditsky
206: © Aleksey Naroditsky
210 (centre right): © Aleksey Naroditsky
212 (left, third from top): © Aleksey Naroditsky
214: © Aleksey Naroditsky
216–17: © Aleksey Naroditsky
220 (top row): © Archives and photo archives from the A.V.
    Schusev State Museum of Architecture
220 (centre left): © M. P. Kudryavtsev, *Moscow: Third Rome*,
    Troitsa Publishing, Moscow, 2008